Write to the Top

Write to the Top®

Writing for Corporate Success

DEBORAH DUMAINE

Random House Trade Paperbacks

New York

2004 Random House Trade Paperback Edition

Copyright © 1983, 1989, 2004 by Deborah Dumaine

LIBRARY OF CONGRESS CATALOGING-IN-PUBLICATION DATA
Dumaine, Deborah.
Write to the top: writing for corporate success / Deborah Dumaine.— 3rd ed.
p. cm.
Includes index.
ISBN 0-8129-6898-0 (trade pbk.)
1. Business writing.   2. English language—Business English.
3. Business communication—Data processing.   I. Title.

HF5718.3.D85 2004   808'.06665—dc22   2003070150

Random House website address: www.atrandom.com

Printed in the United States of America

4 6 8 9 7 5

Book design by Mary A. Wirth

To Mark and Mimi, with enormous gratitude
for your love and support

Acknowledgments

This revision of *Write to the Top* reflects not only my ideas but also the insights and originality of the Better Communications® instructors. Building on the concepts in the first two editions, we are pleased to share our latest techniques and strategies on our 25th anniversary of solving the written-communications challenges of corporations. Our enthusiastic and dedicated team of writing consultants has helped develop the skills of more than 83,000 corporate workshop participants since 1978. They assure us that our consultants' creativity and continuous improvement help them for years after the program.

We have used this book to gather practical document strategies from many worlds: sales, technical, finance, manufacturing, and more. We share here breakthroughs our customers have made—proposal strategies that have won major business for the Fortune 1,000, approaches that have won over irritated customers, and internal e-mail that has driven action.

Many members of the Better Communications team have contributed. My enormous thanks go to the following colleagues:

2003 edition

Larissa Hordynsky is one of the most impressive writers I have worked with over the years. As the lead editor in this revision, she documented, updated, and edited sections reflecting Better Communications' new developments and insights. Larissa is one of those rare writers who can work at both the highest conceptual and most subtle editorial levels with equal excellence. She can always find one more way to improve a manuscript, no matter how many others have approved it.

Writers of model documents for inspiration

Three professionals whom I admire contributed model documents: Jocelyn Bartlett, Diane Bailey-Boulet, and Stephen Hochman.

Special thanks

Marjorie Ringrose, Mark Hochman, and Nancy Lee Nelson for their contributions to designing *Bottom Line Thinking,* a program that has greatly advanced our work in report and presentation writing for the professional-services industry.

Special-entry writer

Bob Cipriano contributed "Write for the Web."

For brainstorming or editing new sections

Marya Danihel was an important sounding board and edited several exercises. As director of Instructional Development at Better Communications since 1998, she has been an invaluable contributor over the years.

Feedback from thoughtful readers

Nancy Lee Nelson, Diane Bailey-Boulet, Miriam Dumaine.

Expert advisors

Sandra Simpson, president and founder of Speaking Like a Pro; Claudyne Wilder, presentations consultant, seminar leader, and president, Wilder Presentations; and Mark Hochman, president, Hochman & Co.

Project director 2003

Lauren K. Terry meticulously managed the manuscript to its completion, cheerfully greeting each new edit and version. Along the way she wrote several imaginative pages herself.

Special thanks to our amazing manuscript team

Elisabeth Healey was tireless in her dedication to accuracy and to the development of new graphics. She was the soul of patience in the face of countless challenges. Jocelyn Bartlett proofread the entire manuscript with impeccable attention to detail. Her insights were invaluable. Thanks also to Paul Kursky for hours of editing and some inventive writing, too.

Manuscript preparation

Elizabeth Lee Nelson: we appreciate her energy and great attitude.

For bringing the message of strategic writing to the world over the years

Thanks to Anne Fiechtner, Dorothy Johnson, Nancy Lee Nelson, Diane Bailey-Boulet, Deborah Daw, and above all, my sister Miriam Dumaine.

Thanks to my editors

For making it possible for me to break into the world of book writing and thus launching my career, Charlotte Mayerson, my first Random House editor. Thanks, too, to Tim Farrell and Judy Sternlight, my 2004 editors, for their patience and enthusiasm.

Earlier editions

For brainstorming, writing, or editing a chapter: Barbara Blanchard, a great writer and friend of Better Communications, Diane Kellogg, Stephanie E. Bernstein, Phyllis Meyer, Patricia Hamilton, Larry Raskin, Deborah White-house, and Joe Kelley.

Editorial assistance

Patricia Hamilton, Jane Evanson, and Marlene Johnson contributed enormously to earlier editions. My continuing thanks go to Sherri Federbush for her help as developmental editor. Others who offered valuable editorial suggestions were Ann Blum, Priscilla Claman, Brian Dumaine, Lisa Danchi, Eve Goodman, Marea Gordett, Karen Horowitz, Alex Johnson, Carolyn Russell, Harry Saxman, Michael Segal, Caroline Sutton, Jenny Webster, Mary Kennedy, and Jessica Forbes.

And finally, thanks to our supporters

The Better Communications staff

—with appreciation from Deborah Dumaine

Contents

What's in This Book?

Write to the Top® is on the shelves of almost 100,000 businesspeople. Most of them first used it in Better Communications'® globally attended workshops and coaching sessions. The response from readers and clients has been most enthusiastic—they tell us that they have improved their ability to drive action through writing. It's been gratifying to gather data showing that our techniques have saved our users time and improved the quality of their documents.

Now we have updated this book to share our newest strategies and latest breakthroughs. We also want to pass along the excitement that comes with mastering one of the hardest parts of most people's jobs.

Good writing is a powerful tool; it can make your message stand out from the mass of materials competing for attention in corporations every day. Good writing focuses your ideas for maximum impact on the reader and helps you get the response you want from your colleagues. Studies show that if you can't write clearly and powerfully, your career advancement will always be seriously limited.

Pressures of the electronic age

The ever greater use of e-mail to grease the wheels of business has galvanized the need for clear and concise writing. Managers don't have the time—or the inclination—to unravel poorly organized material. Whether you're writing a letter, a sales memo, or a detailed financial report, it is crucial that you write lucidly and persuasively. Even the most outstanding idea can be defeated by mediocre writing.

With the expectation that every e-message will get a same-day reply and each proposal will be completed virtually overnight, writing speed is an essential skill today. Every document you write is no doubt a race to the finish. We have been delighted to know that our various step-by-step processes have helped writers increase their writing speed by 30 to 50 percent.

As president and founder of Better Communications, Deborah Dumaine has spent the last 25 years developing writing-improvement techniques specifically in response to the needs of corporate writers. Better Communications has successfully used these methods to develop managers' skills in Fortune 1,000 companies globally.

Common types of business documents

For those of you who are just starting out in business writing, here's a partial list of the most common types of documents we see in our work with clients.

Annual Reports	Proposals	**Often in e-mail form:**
Audit Reports	Requests for Proposals	Minutes of Meetings
Feasibility Studies	(RFPs)	Problem-Solving Memos
Performance Appraisals	Research Reports	Procedural Change Notices
Planning Reports	Sales Letters and Reports	Trip Reports
Presentations	Status Reports	Work Orders
Procedure Manuals	Training Materials	

How to use this book: speed-start guide

Write to the Top is divided into five parts, three of which are new:

> Part 1: Six Steps to Reader-Centered Writing®
> **NEW!** Part 2: Writing Presentation Documents™
> **NEW!** Part 3: Challenges of Persuasion
> **NEW!** Part 4: Action Through Words
> Part 5: Quiz Yourself: Find Your Personal Strengths and Weaknesses

In addition to a brief overview of the five parts, we have provided the following speed-start guide to help you find what you need fast. You don't need to read this book from beginning to end to start writing documents that drive action. Rather, read Part 1 for an introduction to our most popular process, then move to the section that matches the challenge you face.

Speed-Start Guide to *Write to the Top*

For this kind of challenge . . .	. . . and this kind of document . . .	. . . see this section
Making everyday writing clear, concise, and action-oriented	Memos, short proposals, reports, e-mail, letters	Part 1: Six Steps to Reader-Centered Writing
Planning stand-up presentations	Slide shows and collateral material	Part 2: Writing Presentation Documents
Building a logical argument within a document	Research-based reports or proposals, complex recommendation sections in any document	Part 3: Report Credibly Part 2: Writing Presentation Documents
Making a sale	Proposals and sales letters	Part 3: Write to Win Sales® Part 3: Write a Persuasive Proposal
Writing with peers, delegating writing, writing for someone else's signature, editing others, managing a writing team	Any	Part 4: Write as a Team
Writing e-mail that commands attention and generates action	Internal memos, communication with clients and prospects	Part 4: Energize Your E-Mail
Grammar and punctuation self-assessment and practice	Any	Part 5: Quiz Yourself

About the parts of the book

Part 1, which presents the **Six Steps to Reader-Centered Writing,** has been updated to offer more guidance on e-mail and quick-turnaround documents. In Step 1 you'll learn how to begin the writing process by analyzing your audience and defining your purpose. Step 2 explains how to generate ideas and get the writing process started. Steps 3 and 4 involve grouping information and sequencing your ideas for maximum impact on your readers. Finally, Steps 5 and 6 go into detail about writing, then editing your document. We have also added advice on visual design.

In **Part 2** you'll learn about **Writing Presentation Documents,** including that most used and abused tool of the day, PowerPoint®. What are the secrets of persuasion for a stand-up presentation? How do your meet your audience's needs and impress them with your message? How much text is appropriate in slides? What kind of graphics should you use? When is using a flip chart more effective than creating a slide? What handouts should you give your audience? This section will answer all these questions and more.

Part 3: Challenges of Persuasion deals with the challenges of motivating readers to act.

- How long should your report be? In **Report Credibly,** you'll find guidance on writing both formal and informal reports and tips on structuring them to communicate your results convincingly.
- Writing can be a compelling way to build customer interest and to move a sale forward. The principles outlined in **Write to Win Sales** will help you write faster, saving time to make more sales.
- **Write a Persuasive Proposal** will help you win new business and expand ongoing relationships. Respond to your customers' needs and show your own understanding of them in an easy-to-read format. Customers will reach for your proposal first—ahead of your competition's.

Part 4: Action Through Words helps you get the job done at work.

- **Energize Your E-Mail** provides strategies for surviving and reducing information overload. Learn ways to manage the quality, quantity, and strategy of the messages you send.
- The Internet requires a writing style all its own. Our tips on developing, organizing, and editing your message in **Write for the Web** will help you design a Web site that reaches out to your intended audience.
- Writing as a team—even a team of two—is a potential source of frustration and lost productivity. In **Write as a Team,** you'll learn to manage the process efficiently, keeping everyone on track while resolving style conflicts.

- **Give Meaning to Minutes** offers a great model for easy-to-implement meeting reporting and tracking.
- Occasionally, you must resort to writing to give feedback on behavior. **Shape Performance Through Your Writing** offers simple tips on documenting performance problems.
- **Trigger a Response by Letter** gives you a game plan when you need the cooperation of a vendor to resolve a service problem. You'll find advice on how to organize your letter, effectively present your problem, and achieve your desired action.

Part 5: Quiz Yourself helps you with more specific problems of grammar and editing. The Better Communications method divides the writing task into a series of subskills. Here you can pinpoint your individual strengths and weaknesses in each area as you edit and then complete the appropriate self-assessment exercises. Some of your skills may need only a quick review; others may require more serious attention. The on-site workshops we deliver to corporate clients are self-paced and interactive, and the exercises in this book reflect the same approach.

As with most skills, writing is improved primarily by practice. This book offers both guidance and practice exercises to sharpen your writing ability and make this daily task less burdensome. The strategies all work—but only if you do. You must get involved in order to learn. Would you expect to become a competent swimmer simply by reading a book about swimming? Neither will you improve your writing simply by reading a book or listening to a lecture. Here we offer a tested program that asks that you *write* as well as read. Just as swimming laps improves your swimming, every page you actually work on will benefit your writing.

PART ONE

Six Steps to Reader-Centered Writing®

To write simply is as difficult as to be good.

W. SOMERSET MAUGHAM

Writing Can Make
or Break Your Career

Most of us dread writing in some way

Tom LeBlanc glances at his watch and then back at the empty screen in front of him. The ticking of the wall clock grows louder, and a siren outside the window makes him lose his train of thought for the second time. The right words are just beyond his reach.

His mind wanders to the next day's appointments and to the movie he is going to see with Elaine that evening. A ringing telephone brings his attention back to the memo he wants to write. "I'm just not getting anywhere," he thinks. "I know pretty much what I want to say, but I can't get those first words out."

Tom stands, straightens up his desk, and wonders if a cup of coffee will wake him up. "Maybe I'll just let it go until tomorrow," he mutters.

An enormous percentage of the people we work with tell us that they regularly feel the way this manager does. Whether writing a long report or a short memo, they find themselves staring at the blank page or screen more often than they'd care to admit. At those times the process can seem so overwhelming that many will do anything to avoid getting started.

Writers get into this trouble because most of them were not taught an effective, step-by-step approach to writing. They were often told, with bright red pen, what they were doing wrong, but few teachers ever said, "Write this way!"

Convenient distractions

In the office there are many distractions: the phone rings, an associate drops by, or there's e-mail to check. Here is a list of obstacles to writing mentioned by participants in a Better Communications® business-writing workshop:

- I need to clean my desk before I can start writing.
- I can't find the time to do my job and write this proposal, too.
- My manager called a special meeting.
- No matter what I write, it will be ripped to shreds.
- I don't understand why they want me to put this in writing.
- I need to check my messages first.

For those who dread beginning or who are embarrassed about their skills, almost any other activity will win out over writing.

Our mass-media society sabotages good writing skills

These days it's easy to communicate with a minimum of writing. The Internet gives us business information, news, and entertainment. Family, friends, and business associates are a phone call away. E-mail barely counts as writing anymore—much to the detriment of clear communication. People read dramatically fewer books than they did 50 years ago, and it shows. As we read less fiction or nonfiction, we are becoming far less comfortable with the written word.

No wonder many people say that writing is the part of their job they like the least. In fact, most of them would probably be happy to see other methods of communication replace writing completely.

Today's biggest writing challenges

Our clients tell us that they are faced with several challenges that they are aware of. After listing these, we'll add a couple they may *not* be aware of.

No time

The first and most daunting task most businesspeople climbing the corporate ladder experience is the need to write twice as quickly as perhaps five years ago. In a company that has experienced downsizing, these people must be able to do a job that two or three did in the past. If they are slowed down by their writing responsibilities, their daily success and possibly their careers will suffer.

The good news: This book has a solution that works for improving writing efficiency. At Better Communications we measure the writing productivity of over 4,000 graduates each year—and all report writing 30 to 50 percent faster after taking one of our workshops!

Writer's block

The inability to get started can have many causes: not knowing who your readers are or how to approach them, lacking a clear vision of where you want to go with your message, negative past experiences that shook your confidence.

The good news: There are many more causes of writer's block, but our strategies will help you overcome them all. According to our graduates, even years after one of our workshops, their start-up speed keeps improving.

Constant interruptions

It's frequently impossible even to reply to an e-mail without three phone calls and two drop-ins slowing you down. This, on top of the two challenges we have already discussed, can grind you to a halt.

The good news: This book offers several step-by-step processes that can guide you through writing any type of document, from the simplest e-mail to the most complex of presentations. If you are interrupted in Step 3, it's all right. You can go back anytime, finish that step, and move on to Step 4. You always know where you are in the writing process and what to do next.

It's hard to persuade and influence

There are specific techniques for convincing readers that your ideas are the right ones. Some are simple—good for quick e-mails, for example. Others guide you through the process of constructing persuasive arguments built on inductive logic. These arguments can be inserted into more than one type of document.

The good news: You can find strategies for influence and persuasion in this book.

Building your professional image—and your career

There are two challenges of which corporate writers are often blissfully unaware. The first is professional image, how you are perceived by your managers and peers. We are constantly surprised at how many corporate writers, especially emerging ones, don't understand that their casual "instant messaging" approach to business e-mail is doing them a grave disservice. They just don't believe that taking the time to write a professional-sounding e-mail makes a difference. Managers, however, are constantly telling us that they judge others negatively for this failure. Indeed, managers doubt other aspects of their coworkers' skills when they receive careless, error-filled e-mail.

Second, if you work in a large company and are known only on e-mail, you face the challenge of how to differentiate yourself and advance your career. With the ever-greater use of phone and Internet conferencing, many meeting participants have never met one another. Do you judge others a bit harshly if they send you a messy e-mail riddled with errors? Are you sure that yours don't look the same? Do you take the time to use spell check and grammar check?

The good news: "Energize Your E-mail" in Part 4 will help you avoid these all-too-common errors. Part 5 focuses on the rigors of editing and lets you quiz yourself to see how much you already know.

Writing skills will always be vital to business success

Most businesspeople we meet are not happy with their writing skills. On top of this, they spend hours reading and replying to ever more e-mails a day. They must make decisions about graphics and page layout—tasks that are alien to most. No matter how technological the workplace may become, real power will still have its source in the written word.

Good writing skills are in demand by employers. Skill in writing correlates highly with the ability to think well—to analyze information, weigh alternatives, and make decisions. Writing ability is also one of the core competencies necessary to climb the corporate ladder. Our experience consulting with executives verifies that, these days, no one gets to the top without being able to write well.

Why business documents fail

No matter what the topic, most of the writing we coaches and editors see suffers from one major flaw: it is written more from the writer's point of view than from an angle that will appeal to the reader. One of the greatest challenges to writers is to get outside of their personal interests to present their ideas in a way that will answer every reader's four biggest questions:

1. What's this about?
2. Why should I read this?
3. What's in this for me?
4. What am I being asked to do?

We will be explaining more about reader-centered writing and how to achieve it as we go through "Six Steps to Reader-Centered Writing®," "Writing Presentation Documents™," "Challenges of Persuasion," and "Action Through Words." You'll see how the reader-centered approach will make your writing more persuasive and help you achieve the results you want.

Why use a process?

How do efficient writers write? Some seem to have a natural flair, while others develop the skill through practice. Most of the participants in our writing workshops confirm that their writing improves when they begin to look at it as a manageable process, rather than as an irritating chore. How can you make this shift in attitude? By breaking the writing task into its components.

The different steps we offer for various types of documents make efficient writing easy to learn. Using a systematic approach, you can always pick up where you left off in the process, even after an unexpected interruption. This is an especially important skill if you're working on more than one document at a time.

A writing process benefits the writer in surprising ways

One manager wrote a long document developing an idea for a new business direction. As he worked his way through the writing process, he changed his mind about the value of pursuing the new approach and actually recommended aborting the project. "The writing process helped me see the facts more objectively," he told us. Because he had been so emotionally tied to his great idea, he wasn't able to think it through clearly until he systematically approached the task of writing it down.

Writing is thought on paper, a tool for creating and organizing ideas. When writers transfer random ideas from the brain to paper, they begin to understand their own thoughts better. As they continue the process and develop a polished document, they refine their ideas.

Why the emphasis on Reader-Centered Writing?

We've seen people with superb writing skills get poor or apathetic responses from their readers. Why? They were too caught up in their own agenda to put themselves in their readers' shoes. Perhaps they said too much or too little, but whatever the reason, they lost their audience. One of the biggest complaints we get from readers of poor documents is "I don't know what she wants from me."

The phrase "I understand where you're coming from" became popular because communicators of every sophistication level discovered that being other-oriented is the key to getting a message across. Many people practice this technique in oral communication but fail to apply it effectively to the written word.

Here, then, is an outline of the professional business writer's process. The good news: 80 percent of our workshop graduates report that they have cut their writing time by one third. As measured by our assessment tools, the quality of their documents has improved an average of 110 percent. The response from their readership is equally enthusiastic: because documents in *Write to the Top*® style communicate twice as quickly, these readers estimate a 50 percent time savings.

So, are you ready to begin?

It's easy to know *why* to write. The challenge is knowing *how* to reach out to your readers and how to write efficiently. To start, we recommend Six Steps to Reader-Centered Writing for your day-to-day documents, including important e-mail. It's as easy as 1, 2, 3 . . . 4, 5, 6!

The Six Steps to Reader-Centered Writing

STEP 1: **Analyze your audience and define your purpose.**
Use the *Focus Sheet*™.

STEP 2: **Use a Start-up Strategy to generate ideas.**
If you know exactly what you want to say:
Traditional outline or list

To generate ideas:

- Questioning
- Brainstorm Outline
- PowerPoint®
- Post-it® notes or tape, index cards
- Free Writing
- Dictating

⎤
⎥— **PLAN**

STEP 3: **Group information under headlines.**
List headlines—important topics.

STEP 4: **Sequence your ideas.**
Put your bottom line on top (B.L.O.T.)—most of the time.

STEP 5: **Write the first draft.**

A. Quickly write a paragraph for each headline.

B. Add other headlines as more topics emerge.

C. Resist editing until Step 6!

D. Get distance.

⎤— **DRAFT**

STEP 6: **Edit for clarity, conciseness, accuracy, visual design, and tone.**

A. Use the *"Be Your Own Editor" Checklist*.

B. Use *How to Create Visual Impact*.

⎤— **EDIT**

Step 1:
Analyze Your Audience and Define Your Purpose

When you start a letter or e-mail message, you are starting a relationship; you will need cooperation and agreement from the reader for the relationship to work. It's best to begin by knowing what you want and by understanding what the other person expects. The more you consider your reader, the better your chances of getting the response you desire.

Complete the *Focus Sheet*™

To start this relationship, create a reader profile. Although you may not know your readers personally, use your experience to answer some basic questions about who they are and what you want to communicate. The following *Focus Sheet* will help you clarify what you intend to accomplish with your memo, letter, or report and will keep your writing on target. Use the *Focus Sheet* to begin every writing project.

How to answer the questions

By answering the questions on the *Focus Sheet*, you've started planning your document. You are bringing it into focus. Each question is directed at a specific issue that you must analyze as you prepare your document. For example, understanding

- *the reader's role* determines your tone
- *what your reader knows about the subject* determines content and vocabulary
- *how the reader will use the document* influences the format you choose.

Focus Sheet

Answer these questions as the first step in any writing task.

1. Purpose

    A. Why am I writing this? _____

    _____

    B. What do I want the reader to do? _____

    _____

2. Audience

    A. Who *exactly* is my reader? Do I have more than one? _____

    _____

    B. What is the reader's role: Decision maker? Influencer? Implementer? Other? _____

    _____

    C. What does the reader know about the subject? _____

    _____

    D. How will the reader react to my main message: Receptive? Indifferent? Resistant? _____

    _____

    E. What's in it for the reader? Why should the reader read this or agree with it? _____

    _____

    F. How will the reader use this document? _____

    _____

    G. What cultural issues could affect this communication? Ethnic? Corporate? Language? Social? _____

    _____

    H. Should anyone else receive this? _____

    _____

3. Bottom Line

    A. If the reader were to forget everything else, what one main message do I want the reader to remember? _____

    _____

    B. *So what?* What is the impact of my bottom line? _____

    _____

4. Strategy

    A. Should my message be a document? Or would a phone call be more effective? _____

    _____

    B. Timing: Am I too early? Or too late to send it at all? _____

    _____

    C. Distribution list: trimmed to the minimum? _____

    _____

    D. Is someone else communicating the same information? Should I check? _____

    _____

    E. Which method(s) of transmission should I use?

❏ Fax?	❏ E-mail?	❏ Internal mail?
❏ Videoconference?	❏ A meeting?	❏ A presentation?
❏ Internet?	❏ Postal delivery?	❏ Courier?
❏ Intranet (Web sites or shared folders)?	❏ Other? _____	

Let's look at each of the four *Focus Sheet* areas in detail.

Purpose

What are some of your typical reasons for writing? Here are a few:

to persuade	to analyze	to explain
to request	to motivate	to recommend
to present findings	to respond	to praise
to solve a problem	to propose	to announce

Notice that "to inform" does not appear on this list. Very few documents are strictly for the purpose of imparting information. Usually, you want to persuade the reader to act, or at least to agree with you. If you think you are writing to inform, take a second look. Ask yourself if you've analyzed your purpose carefully enough. It should drive action on the part of the reader. This is the reason that the *Focus Sheet* asks "What do I want the reader to do?"

Your purpose should be strategic, not informational. For example, are you writing to inform your manager about your group's progress? Maybe. But isn't your primary purpose really to convince your manager that she can be confident in your leadership?

Make sure you have a strong statement of purpose that drives the action you want—even if it's only a change in attitude.

Audience

In analyzing your audience, consider such questions as:

- Is my audience likely to be receptive, indifferent, or resistant?
- If there are several readers, will their reactions differ?
- How technical can I be?
- What cultural issues could affect this message? For example, do I have a global audience?
- Should I soft-pedal the request, or should I be assertive?

Bottom line

What is the one message you want the reader to remember? The sooner you can boil it down to one or two sentences, the easier it will be to write. If you are having trouble stating your bottom line, continue with the process, then return to this question after Step 2.

The bottom line is often more subtle than you would expect. For example, when you are announcing a meeting, the bottom line is probably not "I'm holding a meeting." It's more likely to be "This meeting is vital to the success of our project!" Don't always go with your first idea.

So what? Why is it important for the reader to take action? And what are the risks of *not* taking action? The "so what?" will drive home the importance of your bottom line.

Strategy

Timing is essential. Should you send it today? In a week? You might defeat your purpose if you submit a controversial proposal an hour before the vice president leaves for a vacation. Or you could be helping your cause if you present it shortly after the vice president has received praise for his trend-setting management techniques.

We often see managers writing much too late to solve problems. Be sure you haven't lost your opportunity to deal with the situation. Writing after the fact wastes both your time and your readers' and has the unintended negative consequence of lowering your credibility.

Also ask yourself if you are the person who should be writing. Would a phone call or other method of communicating be better? What about a meeting, a presentation, or a telephone conference?

Whether e-mailing or sending paper, trim your distribution list to the minimum. Avoid circulating copies of memos unless they really matter to each person receiving them. People will start ignoring you if you send copies indiscriminately. When we ask our executive-level clients for the most important step people might take to improve their written communications, they emphatically reply, "Not writing at all!"

When you determine your strategy, you may decide to build in some accountability, such as:

Action requested

Please respond with your system-improvement suggestions by 3:00 P.M., Wednesday, June 9.

Just keep in mind what results you want and make your requests as clear as possible.

Realistically speaking, will you fill out the whole *Focus Sheet* for every document? Sometimes you might abbreviate the process, but the basic principles—purpose, audience, bottom line, and strategy—apply to everything you write, from the shortest e-mail to the most complex proposal.

Sample: a completed *Focus Sheet*

See how one manager used the *Focus Sheet* to get started with a writing project.

Focus Sheet

Answer these questions as the first step in any writing task.

I. Purpose

A. Why am I writing this? *To propose that we run focus groups to evaluate our new small-business accounts.*

B. What do I want the reader to do? *Organize focus groups, believe that this is a good idea, appropriate a budget for this.*

2. **Audience**

   A. Who *exactly* is my reader? Do I have more than one? *Region 11 VP in charge of small-business accounts and other bank managers.*

   B. What is the reader's role: Decision maker? Influencer? Implementer? Other? *Oversees small-business accounts for our bank, thought leader for new ideas and growth, respected.*

   C. What does the reader know about the subject? *Very well informed about small-business accounts; may not realize it's time to evaluate progress.*

   D. How will the reader react to my main message: Receptive? Indifferent? Resistant? *May be resistant to hiring focus groups due to cost—may prefer cheaper methods.*

   E. What's in it for the reader? Why should the reader read this or agree with it? *Because we want to expand our small-business services and need to know how to improve customer service—focus groups are the best way to learn this.*

   F. How will the reader use this document? *To evaluate if focus groups are the best approach to use as a discussion outline with coworkers about the idea of focus groups in general.*

   G. What cultural issues could affect this communication? Ethnic? Corporate? Language? Social? *No problems in this area.*

   H. Should anyone else receive this? *Region 11 general managers.*

3. **Bottom Line**

   A. If the reader were to forget everything else, what one main message do I want the reader to remember? *Focus groups are the way to evaluate customer satisfaction so far. This will help us keep improving and growing.*

   B. So what? What is the impact of my bottom line? *If our customers are satisfied, we may offer more new services.*

4. Strategy

A. Should my message be a document? Or would a phone call be more effective? _Definitely an e-mail._

B. Timing: Am I too early? Or too late to send it at all? _Now is a good time; they're setting the budgets soon._

C. Distribution list: trimmed to the minimum? _Yes._

D. Is someone else communicating the same information? Should I check? _No, the committee appointed me to make the recommendation._

E. Which method(s) of transmission should I use?

❏ Fax?	☒ E-mail?	❏ Internal mail?
❏ Videoconference?	❏ A meeting?	❏ A presentation?
❏ Internet?	❏ Postal delivery?	❏ Courier?
❏ Intranet (Web sites or shared folders)?		❏ Other? _____

Continuing the process

Now that you have a strong sense of your audience and purpose, you are ready to continue with Step 2, "Use a Start-up Strategy to Generate Ideas."

In the next chapter you will find some strategies to help you pull your thoughts together, even when you're not quite sure what you want to say. Some of the ideas are new; others have helped writers for years. In all our writing workshops, at least one of these strategies has transformed a despairing writer into a born-again communicator, undaunted by the next document deadline.

Step 2:
Use a Start-up Strategy
to Generate Ideas

Getting started is, for most of us, the hardest part of writing. But it need not be. Better Communications' Start-up Strategies help writers develop a more positive attitude toward the beginning phases of writing.

Manage your writing time

Do you sometimes try to write a first draft before you've created a plan? The old "ready, fire, aim" approach? Habits like that are time consuming. As you'll see, writing the first draft will be much easier if you invest time in planning. Doing Steps 1 through 4 of the Reader-Centered Writing process first will make your actual writing and editing faster and easier. Engineers make sketches before they start drafting. Efficient business writers must plan the same way.

Generating ideas

First, you need to write down all of your topics and thoughts where you can look at them. Those great ideas you have while taking a shower, when driving to work, or before falling asleep can be forgotten or discounted until you write them down. In fact, all our Start-up Strategies are aimed at making sure you store your ideas—not in your head but in writing.

In many situations, you are the expert. You know the problem you're facing; you know the possible solutions. The content is in your head; you just need to concentrate on presenting it. In other instances, you may have to conduct research, speak with colleagues or consultants, analyze data, meet with clients, or understand user requirements.

Once you write down your ideas, you can

- see if your information is complete
- decide what to include and what to leave out
- organize quickly and efficiently.

Match the strategy to the task

Different writing projects require different start-up techniques. For a short letter, you may need to jot down only a quick list. Longer documents will almost always require more extensive planning.

As difficult as it may be for you to conquer the blank page or screen, your thoughts flow a lot more smoothly if you use one of these Start-up Strategies:

- traditional outline or list
- questioning
- brainstorm outline
- PowerPoint
- Post-it notes or tape, index cards
- free writing
- dictating

Traditional outline (for all types of writing)

Although many of our clients say that writing a traditional outline fills them with dread, we meet one or two in every workshop who tell us that this tried-and-true method works perfectly well for them. If you're one of the lucky ones who can easily envision a plan for your document, keep using the classic outline.

A sample outline for a proposal to purchase a new software package follows.

A SAMPLE TRADITIONAL OUTLINE

To Propose Purchase of XYZ Software

I. Recommendation: buy XYZ software

II. Why?
- A. Feature 1
- B. Feature 2
- C. Feature 3

III. Benefits of XYZ Software
- A. Saves money
  1. Improves turnaround time
  2. Frees people for other tasks
- B. More professional output

IV. What happens if we do nothing?

V. Experiences of other users: they recommend it
- A. Company X
- B. Company Y
- C. Company Z

VI. Costs are competitive
- A. Financing
- B. Installation
- C. Training of personnel

VII. Potential vendors
- A. Acme
- B. Apex

VIII. Implementation timetable
- A. Installation schedule
- B. Training schedule

IX. Options considered but rejected
- A. Option A
- B. Option B

X. Background
- A. Other investigations on this issue
- B. Current software on hand
- C. Compatibility

XI. Long-term plans
- A. Upgrade capabilities
- B. Potential applications

XII. Summary

Using the traditional outline

In its simplest form, an outline is a list of ideas you want to include in your writing—arranged in a coherent order. If you can generate a "quick-and-dirty" list or outline, you don't need any other Start-up Strategies. Many writers use just headlines and key words to make an outline.

Try using the outline view of your word-processing program to move large blocks of text, assign an outline hierarchy, and promote or demote paragraphs within the hierarchy.

The traditional outline is not very helpful, however, unless you know exactly what you want to say. If you feel stuck sketching out content, try another Start-up Strategy.

Combining the traditional outline with another strategy

The other strategies offered here are in fact pre-outline techniques to bring you to the final outline stage. They are all designed to spark a group of ideas you can then put in the best order (see Step 4). Whether you wish to take these ideas one step further by copying them into traditional outline form is up to you. If you do so, indicate the difference between main topics and subtopics.

Here are a few ways to do that:

1. Use Roman numerals, letters, and Arabic numerals—the traditional approach.
2. Use a decimal system.
3. Mark main ideas with a special character, such as a bullet, an asterisk, or an arrow.
4. Write main ideas in one color and less important ideas in a contrasting color. Use three colors if the list or outline is very complex.

Questioning technique (for letters, memos, and e-mail)

Because you have completed a *Focus Sheet,* you have a clearer picture of your readers, their needs, and their expectations. Using that reader profile, engage your audience in an imaginary dialogue.

How does questioning work?

Questioning is very similar to role playing, except that the writer plays both parts.

1. List questions your readers will need answered about your topic. Include such issues as background, requirements, features, benefits, changes, costs, alternatives, and timing.
2. Write answers under each of the questions. Respond to each one as completely as possible; you can cut and refine content later.

If you can't answer all the questions, you may need more information before you can go further. Don't worry yet about the sequence of topics—you'll be able to shift them around later. Use your questions as temporary headlines to label your information and make it easy to locate.

Questioning helps you define the information you'll need, so you won't have to interrupt your writing for more research. By listing all the questions your reader may ask, you will be spared the embarrassment of distributing an incomplete document and the time wasted answering follow-up queries from your readers.

For example, suppose you are drafting a memo announcing a monthly department meeting. What are some of the questions your reader will ask?

- Where and when is this meeting?
- What will be on the agenda?
- How can I prepare for the meeting?
- Am I *required* to go?
- What if I can't make it?

Answer the questions you've generated, and you're on your way. If you're writing e-mail, just type the questions on the screen and then answer them—this becomes your draft.

Brainstorm outline (for longer memos, reports, and proposals)

"How can I possibly keep track of all my ideas?"

The brainstorm outline allows you to pour out all your ideas without committing yourself in advance as to their relative importance or to the order in which you will ultimately present them. If you find yourself thinking, "I have so many ideas, I just don't know how to begin," the brainstorm outline is for you.

What is a brainstorm outline?

A brainstorm outline is a nonlinear, pictorial way of writing down your ideas and their relationship to one another. Since it opens you up to a spontaneous way of thinking, the brainstorm outline goes beyond the traditional outline. It is especially helpful for writing problem-solving memos because it encourages free association. With this strategy, all your ideas are displayed at once so you can easily see their relationships. Similar thoughts are grouped together.

After you have completed the outline, you will be able to decide which topics are most important by numbering them in the order that you want to discuss them. If you like, you can copy them into an easy-to-follow list or outline.

In our sample traditional outline, we proposed the purchase of new software. Here is the same topic in the form of a brainstorm outline.

BRAINSTORM OUTLINE

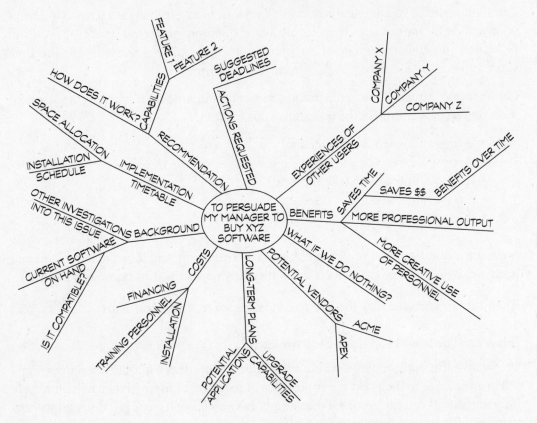

How to plan a report or memo using a brainstorm outline

In the center of a piece of plain white paper or your screen, draw a circle big enough to contain six or seven words. In the circle, write the main goal of your memo or report. Use an action verb

- to persuade
- to propose
- to explain.

Now draw a line extending out like the spoke of a wheel in any direction from the circle. Jot down an important idea on the line. It doesn't matter whether this is the topic you want to mention first or last in the final draft. List all ideas as they occur to you, as quickly as you can. Try to keep the momentum going.

Continue adding spokes for different thoughts. As you write each thought down, ask yourself whether it deserves a spoke of its own or whether it should be an offshoot of an existing spoke. Group ideas about the same subject along the same spoke or one emerging from it.

On your own: Use a brainstorm outline to plan a memo suggesting a change in one of your company procedures that you believe would improve your working atmosphere.

Remember: 1. Put ideas that are related on the same spoke or close to it.
2. Let less important facts branch out from the more important ones.

PowerPoint (for long reports and presentations)

Use the notes-page view of PowerPoint as a Start-up Strategy, especially for presentations. Each notes page reproduces a slide, with half a page of space below for typing text. Give each topic its own page, then use the outline view to sort, organize, and resequence the pages.

You can accumulate a lot of material before deciding on a structure for presenting your message. Shuffle the order of your topics, discard irrelevant ones, and add afterthoughts without wasting valuable time and energy rewriting. Later you will arrange your information into a framework that will form the skeleton of your presentation. Right now you need only concern yourself with gathering the "bones" that will compose it.

Post-it notes or tape and index cards (for long memos and reports)

Here's an update of the old index-card method: try using movable Post-it notes or tape (manufactured by 3M) as a Start-up Strategy. Write each topic on a separate note or strip of tape. You can then rearrange the Post-its as often as necessary. This is a great strategy if you are away from your computer.

How to plan a memo with movable notes or tape

1. Cover a piece of paper with notes or strips of tape four to five inches long. Write a note, phrase, or idea on each note. Include as many notes as you need to cover all your main points. Don't hesitate to put down any idea—no matter how unimportant. You can always weed it out later.

2. When you've finished recording your content, experiment with different methods of development by changing the order of the notes (see Step 4). Rearrange them until the most appropriate sequence emerges. Explore all possibilities.

3. When you get to your first draft, write one paragraph for each note. Some executives we've worked with are so enthusiastic about this method that they use removable tape for all note-taking occasions. By doing this faithfully, they always have instant outlines, ready to expand into full reports.

On your own: Using movable tape or notes, write a memo dealing with the following situation:

You recently interviewed a candidate for an opening in your department. Write a memo evaluating the candidate's strengths and weaknesses. Do you recommend this person for the job?

Free writing (for all types of documents)

From time to time, you may feel too blocked to make a plan or list of any kind. Perhaps you're so intimidated by what others will think of your writing that you get stuck. If this happens, try free writing, a technique that many professional writers use to limber up.

How to do it

Free writing means putting down everything that comes to mind. As in free associating, the goal is to write down any and all ideas, whether or not they are related to your topic. Try not to stop—don't answer the phone, don't get up for a cup of tea, just keep writing—even if you find yourself swearing on paper or writing about things that are off the topic.

Most of us have an internal critic who wants us to struggle with grammar and work at fine-tuning our sentences as we write them. Don't let that inner voice slow you down. Editing or censoring yourself at this stage disrupts the flow of ideas. If you can't immediately find the word you need, leave a blank and go on. Disregard punctuation and sentence structure for now: use fragments, phrases, whatever emerges. Just keep producing words.

How free writing helps

Letting your thoughts range widely on any issues that come to mind—even personal ones—opens the channels for what you are really trying to say. This process helps you transfer vague ideas circulating in your mind into words before they slip away. Once they are in black and white for you to read, others will soon follow.

Free writing helps you get rid of distracting thoughts that may be interfering with the serious writing you are trying to produce. When your mind keeps returning to last night's yoga class or the $50 your cousin owes you, it's better to let all those distractions spill onto the screen, too. Soon the bothersome thoughts will be released and your mind will feel clearer, ready for other tasks. If you remember an errand you must do later, such as picking up a loaf of bread on the way home, jot it down on a separate list. This, too, will liberate your mind.

Free writing is, in a way, like meditating. It removes the pressure to create a perfect product; anything you write down is acceptable. The mere act of writing in a nonstop, unfettered way will give you confidence, and more and more thoughts will emerge. Suddenly, you have developed a rhythm. The pen is moving as if propelled across the page; your fingers are dancing on the keyboard. This rhythm will stay with you—it gets you rolling the way warm-up exercises help you to jog or dance better.

Your plan seems to write itself

Free writing can generate tangible material for you to work with. After allowing all your relevant and irrelevant thoughts to emerge quickly, you will find a good number of salvageable ideas among them. Mark passages or sentences that represent a useful idea. You may be grateful and surprised to see that three pages of free writing have yielded enough information to create the framework for your outline.

Ideas emerging from free-writing exercises can be transferred to other Start-up Strategies for further planning. Put words or phrases on a brainstorm outline, PowerPoint notes pages, or a traditional outline.

The outpouring on p. 28, from a confused and harried Hope, helped her to pull her thoughts together and find a place to start. Looking back at her scribbling, Hope found some useful ideas in it. She circled every word or phrase that seemed salvageable and tried to group similar ideas by numbering them (see Step 3, "Group Information Under Headlines," on p. 31).

Hope used the free-writing exercise twice more, by which point she had generated enough content to make a complete list of topics for her report. She also used the technique to develop some in-depth initial thinking on several of the ideas that emerged in her first free-writing effort. In the end, she had created a clear outline, ready to develop into a first draft.

Another cure for writer's block: free screening

By simply turning down the contrast on your screen, you can turn off your internal critic when you write. As you stare at the darkened screen, begin to free type. Ignore worries about grammar, spelling, punctuation, word choice, or sequence for the moment. After you have drained your brain, turn up the light and see the results. Even if some of it doesn't make sense, you'll still have plenty of usable ideas.

HOPE'S FREE-WRITING WARM-UP

i hate this. why do i have to write this stupid report? i was really looking forward to some reasonable hours for a change. well, maybe this isn't so bad—ten pages ought to do it. okay, so they want to know more about our biggest new customers, Summit and Apex. why? well, i guess so they can compare the companies more easily and analyze our prospects with them. let's see, what do i know about the companies? when i spoke with lynn from Summit, she said that Summit may be an upcoming acquisition target for Acme. hmm, speaking of acquisition targets, i need to stop by that new shoe store this weekend . . . anyway, i should research what pundits are saying about Summit. what else? well, i remember The Journal saying that Summit is one of the most innovative software companies in the industry. also, didn't susan say that Summit was mentioned in ChainGain? something about their latest supply chain updates, i think. if that's true, i should find out how much they're investing in that. okay, what about Apex . . . i know that they underwent a merger last year. in fact, erica said that it was the worst decision the company had ever made, and that a lot of the employees disagreed with the plan. they are coming out with new products, though, which is more than i can say for Summit. i'll have margaret check on the status of their new press releases. hmm . . . should some of this info be in a spreadsheet?

Dictating as a Start-up Strategy

"*Dictating?* When's the last time you saw a Dictaphone? Oh, yes, that dinosaur down the hall still has one . . ." If that's your reaction, think again. Dictation skills are making a comeback with voice-recognition software.

Free talking

Consider dictating as another form of free writing. Call it free talking. Instead of writing down whatever comes to mind, *say* it instead. Free writing lets you "see what you think," and dictating lets you "hear what you think." It gets the ideas out and gives you a chance to sort through your random, unorganized thoughts. Try starting this way:

Say what's on your mind, whether your thoughts are on- or off-topic. Remember, the point is to get warmed up. Don't censor your ideas, and don't stop talking. You'll be surprised to find how many half-formulated yet valuable ideas lurk in the corners of your brain. Time yourself, and see how much you can say in five uninterrupted minutes.

Do you need a transcript?

Use your transcript to help you write your first draft. (Only *very* experienced dictators can produce transcripts close to being a rough draft, with the ideas already grouped and sequenced.)

Dictating alone, without preparing a transcript from the tape, may be helpful enough so that you can move immediately to another Start-up Strategy and write down some of the ideas you've uncovered. But you'll probably want to use a typed version as a starting point.

The blank-page (or screen) syndrome

The chart that follows summarizes the Start-up Strategies we've covered and also gives suggestions for matching each strategy to your particular "blank-page syndrome." Check

The Blank-Page or Screen Syndrome,
or Choosing the Right Start-up Strategy

Symptom	Remedy
You just don't know where to start.	Use **questioning**. Ask yourself the questions your readers will ask. *or* Use **free writing** or **dictating**. Just start writing or speaking, and don't stop until all your thoughts are on paper. Let yourself free-associate. Edit later.
You need to organize and convey a large amount of information and overlook nothing.	Use a **brainstorm outline.** Then number areas in logical order to create a traditional outline. *or* Use **PowerPoint** or **Post-it**s. Write content, then organize.
You are taking notes in the field, interviewing many people. You are covering many subjects.	Put all of your notes on **Post-it**s or **movable strips of tape,** then arrange them in order to create an outline.
You know exactly what you want to say and have a clear plan in mind.	Use a **traditional outline.**

the list of "symptoms" to find which apply to you, then try the "remedy." Also feel free to use the strategy that simply appeals to you most; match your strategy to your personality.

What to do when you're so blocked you're desperate

When all else fails, find someone with a bit of extra time who is willing to help you. Explain that you're struggling with writer's block and that talking over your writing project would help you tremendously.

Using your *Focus Sheet* as a guide, take notes or, with permission, tape-record the conversation. Mention every possible idea you're thinking of including. Ask the person to listen carefully and to question you when something needs clarification. Later, play back the tape and take notes. Add other information that has occurred to you in the meantime.

Step 3:
Group Information
Under Headlines

You've generated the information you need in Step 2. Now it's time to group related content into categories. Once you've done that, you will be ready to sequence the information (Step 4) and to write your first draft (Step 5).

Group content by category

What is a category? Think of a refrigerator. Each section is for a different category of food: cheese goes in the dairy bin, lettuce in the vegetable bin. What would happen if you looked in the fruit bin and found the ice cream? You'd find a disaster. Whoever unpacked the groceries didn't put things in the right categories. It's your job to organize content so that the reader won't find background information—like melting ice cream—in the recommendations section.

Creating categories: what are your choices?

Once you start thinking about grouping information, you'll realize that there are countless possibilities. However, the same general categories for organizing information prove to be useful again and again, no matter where you work. Information seems to fall into predictable categories that we call *generic*. Here are a few samples:

Proposal
Solution
Background information

Request for action
Rationale for action
Observations

Directions or procedure   Scope of investigation
Results (of a study or project)   Analysis of findings
Explanation of a process   Evaluation
Recommendations   Implementation plan
Conclusions   Explanation of cause
Sequence of events   Description of a situation

Sample generic categories for documents

The following lists will help you identify the generic categories commonly used for business documents and may serve as a jumping-off point for your own projects. These lists are not a substitute for your own serious analysis of the information you want to convey. Use them instead as models of good organization.

Typical Categories for Common Memos and E-mail

Meeting Announcement

1. Time and place of meeting
2. Goals of the meeting
3. Agenda
4. Speakers/attendees

5. Background
   - events leading to calling of meeting
   - what you need to know in advance
6. How to prepare for the meeting
7. Contact/person in charge

Status Report

1. Executive summary
2. Project description
3. Current status: progress to date
4. Completion date
5. Successful aspects
6. Problems encountered
7. Planned solutions
   - further information or resources needed
   - opinion needed
   - decision needed
   - request for confirmation of plan

8. A summary of projects completed
9. Other projects still in progress
   - background
   - status
   - forecast of
     a. schedule and completion date
     b. changes
     c. cost
10. Summary

Product Performance Assessment

1. Overview (of results)
2. Process or task analyzed
3. Problems detected
   - description of problems
   - possible causes of problems
4. Suggested solutions
   - people involved
   - cost (if any) involved
   - time involved
5. Comparison with previous model
   - similarities
   - differences
6. Dates for changes to be made
7. Date of next evaluation
8. Summary

Solving a Problem

1. Problem description
2. Recommended solution
3. Recommendation justified
4. Background
   - symptoms
   - causes
5. Alternative solutions
   - strengths and advantages
   - weaknesses and disadvantages
6. Implementation plan
7. Summary
   - problem restated
   - recommendation restated
8. Next steps

Purchase Request

1. Overview
2. Recommendation (state what you want)
3. Supporting arguments
   - Why? Predicted productivity improvements
   - Why? Best price
   - Why? Depreciation benefits
   - Why? Reliable brand
   - Why? Competitive advantage
4. Implementation considerations
   - timetable
   - plan
5. Staffing requirements
6. Background
7. Summary

Request for Proposal

1. Overview
2. Service/item required: comprehensive specifications
3. Background
   - concerns and needs
   - how the need arose
4. Possible problems
5. Budget considerations
6. Outline of response needed
7. Deadline for submission
8. Contact person
9. Summary

Proposal

Formal proposal: See Part 3

Letter proposal: See Part 3

Decision-Needed Memo

1. Overview
2. Issue under consideration
3. Recommended action
   - who is involved in the action
   - schedule of steps to take
   - pros and cons
   - subsequent meetings
4. Background: why it became an issue
5. Other decisions/options: pros and cons for each
6. Results of study
7. Summary

How to group ideas from your Start-up Strategy

Traditional outline

If you used a traditional outline in Step 2, you'll have a head start on Step 3. Your ideas are already grouped together. At most, you'll probably find yourself adding subcategories under the Roman numerals or letters.

PowerPoint

If you used PowerPoint notes pages, use the outline or slide-sorter view to organize your pages into groups of similar or closely related topics. Perhaps several of your ideas relate to "reasons for a price hike now." Group all of them together. Other ideas may be part of the implementation plan; group them separately.

Post-it notes or tape, index cards

If you preferred Post-it notes or tape, sort your notes into piles or groups of similar ideas. Do the same for index cards. For each pile or group, think of a one- to four-word "bin"—

a category that will "hold" your ideas. Write that category on a Post-it or tape strip and attach it at the top of each list.

Brainstorm outline

If you chose a brainstorm outline as your Start-up Strategy, you may have done much of your clustering as you brainstormed. The spokes of your outline are your main categories, while the side branches are the subcategories. Look for big-picture categories, and draw circles around your major segments. If you need to include more than one spoke in your circle, that's fine.

During Step 4, when you sequence your ideas, you will number the spokes in the order that you will present them in your final document. If your outline is complex, circle numbered areas in different colors. Here is our brainstorm outline with the ideas sequenced (though you may prefer another, equally good sequence).

BRAINSTORM OUTLINE WITH CATEGORIES CLUSTERED

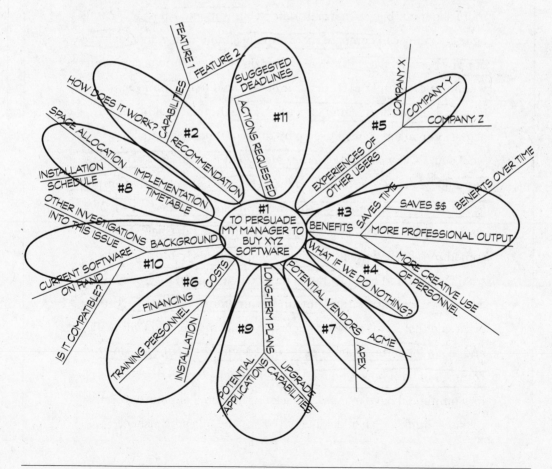

Free writing

If you used free writing to start, you can organize your ideas as we have done in Hope's example.

1. Subdivide your writing into categories by circling ideas you want to use. Discard the rest.
2. Use colored circles to group closely related ideas.
3. Make a separate list of the categories.

HOPE'S FREE-WRITING WARM-UP, WITH IDEAS CIRCLED

i hate this. why do i have to write this stupid report? i was really looking forward to some reasonable hours for a change. well, maybe this isn't so bad—ten pages ought to do it. okay, so they want to know more about our biggest new customers Summit and Apex why? well, i guess so they can compare the companies more easily and analyze our prospects with them let's see, what do i know about the companies? when i spoke with lynn from Summit, she said that Summit may be an upcoming acquisition target for Acme hmm, speaking of acquisition targets, i need to stop by that new shoe store this weekend . . . anyway, i should research what pundits are saying about Summit what else? well, i remember The Journal saying that Summit is one of the most innovative software companies in the industry also, didn't susan say that Summit was mentioned in ChainGain? something about their latest supply chain updates, i think. if that's true, i should find out how much they're investing in that okay, what about Apex . . . i know that they underwent a merger last year in fact, erica said that it was the worst decision the company had ever made, and that a lot of the employees disagreed with the plan they are coming out with new products, though, which is more than i can say for Summit. i'll have margaret check on the status of their new press releases. hmm . . . should some of this info be in a spreadsheet?

4. Pinpoint a word or phrase that categorizes each group. For example, is it a summary? A list of benefits? Write that word or phrase at the top of the appropriate group.

No matter which Start-up Strategy you chose, you'll end up with a list of categories. This is in fact your rough outline, ready to be fleshed out and put into sequence.

Use headlines: go public with your categories

By clustering and organizing your ideas, you've built a framework for your document just as if you were building the frame of a house. The next task is to use that framework or outline to help your readers. Rather than making them guess whether they are reading background or the problem statement, share your outline. Translate your generic categories into specific headlines designed to guide your readers through your document.

First, what is a headline?

The five words you just read are a headline. They illustrate the content of the paragraph that follows by converting general categories to more specific and informative words. The primary difference between categories and headlines is that headlines are used as a device in a written document, and they are often more specific. "Background" as a headline wouldn't be as helpful as "We've never had a policy on early retirement."

While categories tend to be universal, it would be boring if all documents repeated the same headlines you previously saw in "Typical Categories for Common Memos and E-mail." It's much more helpful to readers to replace generic labels with catchy and specific headlines that accurately reflect the content of the paragraph.

Headlines meet the need to organize large amounts of information meaningfully and allow the reader easy access to content. Out of sheer necessity, headlining is rapidly becoming the writing approach of choice.

Are headlines necessary for every document?

Most emphatically, yes. Today's readers are too busy and distracted to read every word, even in a short e-mail, carefully. Headlines show readers what is important to them. They are the natural solution to information overload.

See for yourself how headlines help, even in e-mail

Two e-memos follow. Don't read them; just glance at them. Which do you like better?

From: cnovak
Sent: Monday November 21, 2020 12:23 PM
To: mbanks
Subject: **Collection Inefficiency**

This communication is in response to ZAPEX's desire to improve collection efficiency. The accounts receivable operation at ZAPEX Corporation has been reviewing the merits of consolidating its collection activities. To support enhancement of the centralized collection concept and improve performance, the I.T. Department was asked to assist in the evaluation of activities at one of our collection centers to determine its viability as a potential candidate for using digital imaging technology.

The study of current work processes at the Eastbranch Collection Center indicates that employee productivity and the quality of the collection process are impaired by a paper-intensive environment. The implementation of an imaging system that will provide ZAPEX with the capability for improved information management, increased efficiency, and additional control of factors critical to collection activities is recommended by I.T.

Digital imaging applications have been beneficial in environments where paper is the medium on which information is retained. Paper-intensive systems traditionally are labor intensive, fail to meet most auditor requirements for security, are not integrated with computer-based systems, and are difficult to manage and control. I.T. proposes to tailor a customized imaging system to ZAPEX's business requirements enabling collection clerks to reduce time spent on delinquent cases, collect more money, control the work-flow process, and reduce the risk of lost files and their contents.

At this point in time, established performance levels do not exist for present systems and procedures, and centralized collections are new to ZAPEX's collection activities. Before the imaging system is installed, I.T. will measure current performance levels of the operation and determine new levels for the imaging system. After the imaging system has been in production for eight months, I.T. will measure the performance levels again. If the imaging system meets the predefined performance levels, implementation of similar systems in the remaining collection centers will be approved by ZAPEX.

The continued cooperation and support of all personnel involved in this endeavor will be mandatory for its success, particularly in the areas of training and technical support. There are risks inherent in any new system that involves training people in new technology. To safeguard against any potential failures, I.T. will be firmly committed to the provision of technical support and training whenever the requirement arises. Please do not hesitate to call if further information is required.

From: cnovak
Sent: Monday November 21, 2020 12:23 PM
To: mbanks
Subject: **Proposal to improve the accounts receivable collection system**

For the last six months, I.T. has worked closely with thea Accounts Receivable unit at ZAPEX Corporation to review their collection efficiency. Our departments created an internal task force to explore how ZAPEX could

- improve the efficiency of its collection operation
- enhance its ability to provide superior customer service.

Paper-based system hampers efficiency

CRITICAL ISSUE: In its joint study of the Eastbranch Collection Center, the task force found the current paper-intensive system to be inefficient, time consuming, and error prone. The paper files are also vulnerable to destruction and loss.

I.T.'s solution: install digital-imaging technology

To correct these problems, I.T. proposes creating a customized digital-imaging system that will provide the following measurable benefits:

1. Your unit will increase money collection by more than 15%.
2. Management will easily monitor productivity through system-generated reports.
3. The system will meet security and auditing requirements.
4. You will reduce the risk of losing files.
5. Users will have simultaneous access to the same files.
6. You will be able to store active and archived files in a central location.

Why choose I.T. to create and install this technology?

We have a proven track record for designing and implementing major stand-alone systems that are cost efficient and user friendly (see attached successes). Please talk to Paul Kelley or Janet Gonzalez, who have greatly appreciated our problem solving. Since we know our business inside and out, we can offer you superior, convenient service—just down the hall!

Implementation overview

1. Before installing the system, I.T. and Accounts Receivable will measure performance levels of the current operation and determine new levels for the imaging system.
2. I.T. will then develop and install a pilot digital-imaging system at the Eastbranch Collection Center. We will complete the installation within five months.
3. Eight months after the imaging system begins production, I.T. and Accounts Receivable will remeasure the performance levels.

4. If the pilot imaging system meets predefined performance levels, I.T. will develop and install hardware and software for all other collection centers.

Our partnership for success

This system will be as good as the people using it. To help you foster a teamwork environment, we will provide training and intensive technical support to your people. Working together, we can ensure the success of this project.

I'll call soon to schedule a convenient time to discuss this proposal further.

You probably chose the second version, with headlines and bullets that create visual impact and make e-mail easier to read. (We'll explain more about this in Step 6.) Equally important, however, is that *content* has more impact when you use headlines.

Headlines help the reader get the message

Headlines make ideas leap off the page. Notice how the headlines in this book speed up your reading. Thanks to headlines, readers who are in a hurry can skim through a document and zero in on the section that interests them. Although you may have toiled over every sentence, your readers may not have the time or the inclination to read everything you've written.

Headlines make information easier to find

Readers are generally looking for something specific. It is your job to help them find it. Headlines make it easier for your readers to find the section that applies to them or to relocate on second reading a section they found particularly important.

Think how grateful you would be to find in the files a well-headlined report on a subject that you're researching. You could sift through it instantly to find the content you need. Readers appreciate it when the information they are looking for is as easy to find as in the morning paper. Can you imagine a newspaper without headlines?

Can I use my categories as headlines?

Yes. Sometimes the generic category is a good choice. "Solution" may be all you need for a recommendation that is long, complex, and hard to sum up in a phrase. But don't use generic categories to the exclusion of specific ones. To set yours apart from the other documents in your reader's in-box, make your headlines interesting.

Combine the generic with the specific

To give as much information as you can in the headline, it can be useful to include both the generic category and a specific description. Here are two examples:

BACKGROUND: Union growth in Eastern Europe

PROPOSAL: We need to hire a new staff accountant

Step 6 offers more instruction on rewriting headlines for impact. For now, let's try an exercise to make sure you've got the basics. You're an environmental consultant who has just conducted an initial investigation at Apex, Inc. You're reporting your findings to your manager, who will then suggest a course of action to Apex.

Practice writing headlines

Directions: To test your skill in categorizing information, write an appropriate headline in each blank space in the following memo.

Date: January 4, 2010
To: James King, Senior Consultant
From: Amy Stein, Associate
Subject: **Study needed at Apex**

A recent survey revealed a 23 percent increase in employee absenteeism during the past 10 months. The increase occurred exclusively in the 4 departments that moved 10 months ago from the main building to the newly constructed Jarvis Wing. Supervisors in these departments also report a noticeable decline in productivity since the move.

In light of these findings, I recommend that we propose an extensive environmental study of the Jarvis Wing. Some items that warrant investigation are

- noise levels
- quality of lighting
- temperature and humidity.

- Apex, Inc. is legally responsible for providing a hazard-free, ergonomically safe work environment for its employees.
- The operation and productivity of Apex, Inc. depend on the efficient functioning of the departments located in the Jarvis Wing.
- Employee retention depends in part on providing a comfortable work environment.

In response to the increase in absenteeism, I worked with the Human Resources Department to survey the managers of the four departments located in the Jarvis Wing. We made the following observations:

• Employees seem to have trouble hearing telephone conversations.
• Many employees have brought in their own lamps from home.
• Some employees have started using heaters or humidifiers at their desks.

Please let me know by this Friday how you would like to proceed with this client. Apex, Inc. is eager for our help with this problem.

Now compare your answers with the ones that follow. Don't worry if they are not exactly alike. If your headlines match in meaning, you're on the right track.

Problem: Absenteeism increasing

We recommend a study

Implications: Why is this important?

We conducted a survey *or* **Results of questionnaire**

Deadline: Friday *or* **Plans required by Friday**

In conclusion

You've clustered your ideas into generic categories and assigned headlines to each category. Now let's move on to Step 4—how to sequence your sections for best results.

Step 4:
Sequence Your Ideas

One of the most challenging aspects of the writing process is sequencing: putting your ideas in the best order for impact. When you've chosen the appropriate method of development, your readers will be drawn to your ideas.

Choose a method of development (M.O.D.)

All writers need to package their ideas logically. Step 3 covered the framework of the package. Step 4 covers the sequence of ideas within the package. Your *Focus Sheet* will help you choose a method of development (M.O.D.), which then determines the sequence of your paragraphs. Here are the most common methods of development:

1. Order of importance
   a. Most important to least important
   b. Least important to most important
   c. The "bad-news sandwich"
   d. Opinion-reasons *or* reasons-opinion
2. Chronology
3. Process
4. Organization in space
5. Comparison/contrast

6. Specific to general *or* general to specific
7. Analysis
8. Process

Some of these M.O.D.s may overlap a bit, or you may find yourself using different ones in different sections, especially in long documents. It is perfectly acceptable to combine methods of development.

Why is it essential to sequence your ideas strategically?

Clear writing is a sign of clear thinking. If you can put your thoughts together logically, your reader will more likely be convinced that you know what you're talking about. On the other hand, your mental disorganization will be quite obvious once it's spread across a sheet of paper.

Now your hard work creating headlines pays off. If you didn't categorize your ideas with headlines during Step 3, you will have difficulty sequencing them in Step 4. For example, how can you decide if "Background" goes toward the beginning or end of your report if you haven't defined that section by labeling it? This is why headlines are so helpful: they let you see your ideas in movable chunks.

How to choose a method of development

1. Think back to Steps 1 through 3. Remember when you pinpointed your "bottom line" on the *Focus Sheet*? From Step 1 on, you must keep in mind what you really want to accomplish. This is particularly vital in a memo about a controversial subject. Look over the information you've accumulated during your Start-up Strategy (Step 2) and your list of headlines (Step 3). Your key point may easily be under any of the following headlines:

Recommendations	**Action requested**
Deadline	**Decision needed**

2. With your key point in mind, match your sequence to your audience's attitude. Ask yourself:
   - Do I need to persuade my readers, or do they already agree with my viewpoint?
   - Which part of my message is most important? Least important?
   - Do my readers need a neat summary, or is an in-depth analysis more appropriate?

In other words, choose a method of development according to the needs of your reader, your purpose for writing, the nature of your subject and your document, and the way your ideas naturally hang together. The following explanation will help you choose.

M.O.D. #1: Order of importance

A. Most important to least important: bottom line on top

We begin with this method because it is the best organization for almost all documents. If you want your readers to remember your bottom line, you'd better lead with it. You'll find this M.O.D. particularly useful in memos or reports that describe findings or offer important recommendations. In most cases a reader's attention is completely focused only in the first few paragraphs; after that, concentration begins to flag.

Sample headlines

Below are segments that might appear in a typical two-page e-mail or memo. They are arranged in order of importance, from most to least, using questions for headlines. The purpose of this memo is to persuade the reader (who is receptive to your suggestions) to adopt a new approach for improving sample testing procedures.

Our current methods are not working	Describe the problem
How can we improve them?	Offer your recommendation
What are the benefits?	Give background/supporting data
Can we implement the change?	Outline a workable process
What are the next steps?	List action items

This sequence builds support for the recommendation by offering it early, then justifying it. Your audience is not forced to wait until the end of the e-mail for the recommendation. With this logical presentation, the reader has not only a picture of the department's problems but also a road map leading to improved sample testing.

Try this

What changes would make the following e-mail message more persuasive?

From: cduarte@ssns.com
Sent: Tuesday, May 25, 2020 12:34 PM
To: pkresge@ssns.com
Subject: **Review of SSNS 2.0**

Pat,

I have been unsuccessful in my recent attempts to consolidate and move forward our team commitments from the SEPA review of SSNS 2.0. I expect that resource issues may be at the heart of this difficulty.

To refresh the community mind, we have two major commitments regarding telemetry and interim management of SSNS 2.0:

1. Consolidation of ping scripting and reporting between NOVA and the Communications COE.
2. Development of a "null" transaction-based monitor to be positioned in the Data Center and leveraged to monitor MVS subsystem response and availability.

We had all agreed that these two items, in particular, were crucial to the success of SSNS 2.0 in the interim period before a comprehensive network management system was put in place.

At this point, it is imperative we convene to reaffirm our commitments to these deliverables, identify constraints, and set a time frame for their completion that we can report to Ralph (and he will definitely ask when he reads the review).

Chris

How did you do?

You're right if you put the content of the last paragraph first. In its current state, the e-mail is a mystery message: the reader doesn't find the most important information until the end. On first reading, the message seems like a history of the project.

What other changes did you make?

You probably added a headline for each paragraph; that would be a major improvement. Did you also use a more precise subject line than "Review of SSNS 2.0"? The introduction would have more impact if it said, "Meeting to break through project roadblocks." You should also suggest a meeting time, perhaps under the headline "Next step."

Remember: Whenever possible, put your most important information at the beginning of your document, either in summary or in complete form. Using the most-important-to-least-important sequence, or "bottom line on top," you will take advantage of your readers' complete attention at the beginning of the document to get across your key points.

M.O.D. #1A is useful for: announcements, audit reports, lab reports, presentations, problem-solving memos, procedural-change notices, progress reports, proposals, research reports, sales letters and reports, status reports, trip reports, trouble reports.

B. Least important to most important

Understanding your audience's attitude is the key to successful writing. How will your readers react to your message? Sometimes your suggestion, request, or conclusion is just too problematic to use as an opener. A new hire, for example, might mean depriving another group of much-needed resources. Perhaps your memo proposes an unexpected solution to a problem or a controversial request. Some readers, especially from a culture different from yours, may find a forthright, up-front request impolite or abrasive.

If you fear your readers will stop reading when they see bad news, you will have to be more subtle by holding back your bottom line and laying the groundwork first. Perhaps you need "convincers" to lead the readers through your ideas until you bring them around to your point of view.

Bear in mind, however, that a document written in least-important-to-most-important order rarely works well. It's too indirect and potentially irritating: what is the writer leading up to? A more reader-centered variation follows—the bad-news sandwich.

C. The bad-news sandwich

If you're delivering bad news, you probably shouldn't put your bottom line on top, however important it may be. It's better to approach your reader gently, leading up to your bad news so that it won't come as a shock or provoke anger. Then, after delivering bad news, it's ideal to end on a positive note as long as it's genuine—people will be irritated by false-sounding cheerleading.

In some cases, you can "sandwich" your bad news between two pieces of good news on the same topic. For example, suppose your sales prospects are bright for the next quarter even though the numbers are down this month. Moreover, you have plans for coaching salespeople to make them more successful.

But what if you have *no* good news? In that case, you can lead up to a controversial announcement or recommendation by demonstrating the need for it. For example, begin

---

by using a specific instance to describe a problem—and then show how implementing your recommendation can prevent the situation from occurring in the future.

Suppose that you manage a facility where a near accident occurred. It could have been very costly for the company. In writing a request to purchase new safety equipment that exceeds your budget, you would first describe the near accident and then show how the equipment you recommend would prevent it from happening again. You could then close your message on a proactive note suggesting next steps and safety outcomes.

If possible, appeal to mutual interests and emphasize common ground when you're writing about a controversial topic. Try to answer the reader's question, "What's in it for me?"

If you truly can't find a positive fact, at least offer a positive tone. Start with a personal or friendly note before going to the hard issues. End with supportive, action-oriented statements, offering help if possible. At a minimum, show that you understand and care how the bad news will affect the reader.

An example of a bad-news sandwich

What if a manager named Rick had to inform his people that their plant would be closing? Look at his first attempt, the "before" memo on p. 49.

Rick made two mistakes:

1. arranging the information from most to least important from *his* viewpoint
2. emphasizing *his* purpose and goal rather than his *readers'* concerns.

Next look at Rick's "after" memo on p. 50. The information in this one is presented in a bad-news sandwich.

Which memo did you prefer?

Which would be most easily accepted? Which one shows an understanding of people's needs? In the second memo, the appealing and persuasive information is at the beginning, where it will help readers feel positive about potentially disturbing news. The second memo is clearly better.

D. Opinion-reasons or reasons-opinion?

Whenever we consider the issue of most to least important, the question of how to present conclusions and evidence arises. To present information persuasively, state your opinion or theory first, then prove it with supporting evidence. Your opinion will have more impact if the evidence that follows really upholds it. This approach also dramatically increases reader comprehension.

Date: July 10, 2020
To: Alpha plant staff
From: Rick Martinez
Subject: Alpha plant

Alpha plant closing

The Alpha plant has served us well since 1982, but its equipment is becoming increasingly obsolete in these days of nanotechnology. Therefore the company has decided to close the Alpha plant at the end of our fiscal year, September 30, 2020.

All our Alpha plant employees will be offered employment opportunities in our Beta and Gamma plants. Accepting a job in another plant will require relocation. The company has instituted a policy to help with relocation costs. Please consult the Web site for details.

Interview schedule

The Beta and Gamma plant managers will be conducting interviews at our facility the week of July 20. If you are interested in relocating to either the Beta or the Gamma plant, consult the job openings on our Web site and sign up for an interview online.

Retraining

Since the Beta and Gamma plants are more state of the art than the Alpha facility, some retraining may be necessary. You will be informed whether your current skills fit your new job description once we have found you a position at Beta or Gamma.

Rest assured that we value all our employees and hope to welcome you all to the Beta or Gamma plants in October.

To decide whether you should present opinion-reasons or reasons-opinion, consult your *Focus Sheet.* How did you answer the question "How will the reader react?" Choose the appropriate presentation. Just be careful not to lose your proposition by burying it somewhere in the middle.

A case history: what's your strategy?

Should Miriam present her opinion first and reasons later, or vice versa? What does she really want to accomplish? Here's what happened:

For a long time, Miriam and all the other top managers had felt that Rob Martinez deserved a promotion and a raise. His sales figures were the highest at GigaTrix, and he had even started a sales-training program to share his successful strategies.

Date: July 10, 2020
To: All Alpha plant employees
From: Rick Martinez
Subject: Your future at Megatrix

Helping Megatrix change with the times

As you know, Megatrix Corporation has been around since 1982. One of our major assets has always been our adaptability, which has allowed us to gain new clients and stay on the cutting edge. We have maintained our position as a major player in a world of ever-changing technology. To keep Megatrix growing, we need your continued help and understanding—it will pay off for all of us.

Are *your* skills keeping up with the times?

We are offering all of you here at our Alpha plant the opportunity to move to our state-of-the-art Beta and Gamma facilities. Such a move will allow you to update your skills and work with the newest technology. Both you and the company will gain a competitive edge. Once you have been matched with a new position, the company will provide the training you need to help produce our newest and most profitable product line.

What about the Alpha plant?

As some of you may have heard already, Alpha plant equipment is becoming increasingly obsolete in these days of nanotechnology. Alpha has served us well, but it is time to move on. The company has decided to close the Alpha plant at the end of our fiscal year, September 30, 2020. The skills needed to run the Alpha plant will become less and less valuable in the job marketplace.

How the company will help with your transition

Accepting a job at Beta or Gamma will obviously require relocation. Since we are eager to retain you and ease your transition, we have instituted a policy to help with relocation costs. Please consult the Human Resources Web site for details. We are committed to making your learning and transition as successful as possible.

Next steps

Beta and Gamma managers will be conducting interviews here at Alpha the week of July 20. If you are interested in relocating to either the Beta or the Gamma plant, consult the job openings on our Web site and sign up for an interview online.

We hope that all of you will take advantage of the opportunity to move with us. Please continue to help us grow!

Rob's friend Ed had recently hinted to Miriam that Rob was feeling discontented at GigaTrix, but no one believed he would actually leave. Then Miriam found a copy of Rob's updated résumé in the copy machine and realized Ed knew more than he was telling. It was time to write a letter asking the president to grant Rob a long-overdue promotion immediately.

In her memo Miriam chose to present her reasons first and her opinion last. Why? Because she knew that the president, who was on an austerity campaign, would not read beyond the words "salary increase." First, she had to alert him to Rob's possible resignation and remind him of his value to the company. Rob was too important an asset to lose.

In this way Miriam engaged the president enough so that he read the entire contents of her startling memo. Had the economic state of the company been better and had the president been in a spending mood, Miriam could have opened with her opinion and, with luck, secured Rob's promotion.

Test your sequencing ability

Try this brief review to be sure you're prepared to sequence your next document.

When my audience is:	Put the bottom line:
Receptive	_____ *where?*
Indifferent	_____ *where?*
Resistant	_____ *where?*
Unknown	_____ *where?*

How did you do?

If your audience is receptive or unknown, put the bottom line on top. If your audience is indifferent, you have little to lose by stating your point first. If your audience is resistant, you might want to pave the way tactfully to your point, but get there as soon as you can.

Workshop participants have told us that if they don't find the point immediately, they flip to the end anyway. So why hide your message?

Remember: Whenever possible, state your bottom line on top, or as our facilitators like to say, "B.L.O.T."

Audiences with mixed attitudes

If you have only one reader, it's fairly easy to determine the approach you should take. But what happens when you have two or more readers, and one of them loves your ideas, while the other reader is resistant? How do you then sequence your ideas?

If several readers have an equal role in the decision-making process, you will have to treat your audience as hostile and present your ideas accordingly. If, however, they are *not* all equal decision makers, write for the ones who have the power, not the resisters.

How is your document going to be used? Is the reader going to take action or just pass the proposal along to someone who may then give it to yet someone else? If this is the case, be sure you address the concerns of the reader at the end of this chain. Consider this person carefully. She may be the one you have to reach if you really want action.

M.O.D. #2: Chronology

When you need to explain how a product or situation developed, use a chronological M.O.D. Progress reports, meeting minutes, and test procedures are typically arranged in time order. The facts associated with each event or change will structure your plan.

Chronological development presents two major problems. First, the time order may force important material to appear in an unemphatic position—such as the middle. Unimportant issues may get unwarranted emphasis by appearing at the beginning and end. In this case, state the most important idea or recommendation at the beginning, ignoring time association. Then shift to chronological development. It saves the hurried reader time digging out pertinent data.

Second, chronological order can be monotonous. Don't begin each sentence with a date or a string of *next*s. Vary your sentences by using transitional phrases like "after completing the beta test" and "turning to the next phase of the project." It will be easier to hold the interest of your reader.

M.O.D. #2 is useful for: accident reports, lab reports, manufacturing and scientific procedures, minutes of meetings, performance appraisals, planning reports, procedure manuals, progress reports, trip reports.

M.O.D. #3: Process

Unlike the chronological method, which describes an event that has already happened, processes require you to impose your own sequence. With the process M.O.D., you present your material as if you were writing instructions or a recipe. This method of development is useful for explaining a chemical process or how to build, install, operate, or repair a piece of equipment.

Write up the steps of a procedure in a numbered list, in table form if possible. Make sure you thoroughly understand the task you are describing so that each step appears in the correct order.

M.O.D. #3 is useful for: handbooks, lab reports, manufacturing and scientific procedures, procedure manuals, requests for proposals (R.F.P.s), technical reports, training materials, user manuals.

M.O.D. #4: Organization in space

When you're dealing with different geographic locations or describing an object, organize your writing in a sequence that's easy for the reader to follow. You may be delivering statistics in a report that starts with the East Coast and moves across the country to the West Coast, or by your company's sales-office locations. Begin by explaining the order in which you will be covering these areas, and discuss each one completely before moving on to the next.

Spatial order isn't just about geography, by any means. You can use it to describe details on a piece of equipment from left to right, top to bottom, or exterior to interior. Be sure to create a coherent and concrete order that's easy to follow. It's like playing connect the dots. You're given the dots—can you create a clear picture? (Unlike a child's dot-to-dot book, however, your report may have more than one structure that works.)

As you lead your readers from point to point, you create a visual image for them. Make it concrete by adding a graphic—a map, or a drawing of the object—and keying your headlines to map locations or parts of the mechanism.

Remember: Spatial organization in long reports can be just as monotonous as the chronological method. Make a conscious effort to engage your reader by highlighting what's new, special, or significant about your research, mechanism, or trip. Vary your sentence structure.

M.O.D. #4 is useful for: development reports, handbooks, patent applications, market-research reports (by specific company division, district, east-west, country), technical reports, trip reports, user manuals.

M.O.D. #5: Comparison/contrast

Comparison is a technique for juxtaposing items or concepts to emphasize their similarities; contrast emphasizes differences. This M.O.D. is also useful for discussing advantages and disadvantages.

For example, you may be asked to study and evaluate two possible sites for your new downtown office. If there are more advantages than disadvantages, first present all the advantages of the two sites. Then present the disadvantages of both. Don't confuse your readers by mixing statements about advantages and disadvantages in the same section. Arrange your comparison this way:

1. Advantages: Site A and Site B
2. Disadvantages: Site A and Site B

Instead of:

1. Site A: advantages and disadvantages
2. Site B: advantages and disadvantages

Be coherent in your comparisons by using key phrases, such as:

on one hand	the former	in the same way
on the other hand	the latter	although that is true
on the contrary	in opposition to this	
in contrast	but then	

Comparisons are valuable for explaining the unfamiliar to your reader by relating it to the familiar. When comparing two subjects, always mention the more familiar one first. This is the best way to help the reader understand the lesser-known subject. For example, if you're introducing new software, start with a familiar program or service for comparison. Alien ideas have often been understood by comparison: Native Americans called the first trains "iron horses."

Beware of comparing too much technical information in writing. Use a table or chart instead.

M.O.D. #5 is useful for: feasibility studies, market research, planning reports, presentations, proposals, sales letters, technical reports.

M.O.D. #6: Specific to general or general to specific

This M.O.D. helps you instruct or persuade your reader. Should you start with a specific statement and expand it to explain or justify a general idea? Or begin with a general statement and follow with logically linked examples and supporting statements? Refer to the audience analysis in your *Focus Sheet*. Your readers' prior knowledge of and receptivity to your topic will help you choose a sequence.

For example, what if you had to explain a camera to a caveman? He probably wouldn't show a bit of interest in the little silver box unless you first presented the specifics: a snapshot of his spear, a pictorial record of his hunting prowess, and—most remarkable—a picture of his clan. You would be leading him from understanding specifics to the generalized idea: camera.

On the other hand, what if you were explaining the innovations of the latest digital model to an expert photographer? Obviously, you'd start by mentioning the camera and then proceed to describe its specific new features. The photographer already knows what a camera is, so it makes sense to open with it. You're starting with something familiar to orient her to the subsequent new information about the camera's special options.

To review, your readers' knowledge of your subject is the best indicator of which version of this M.O.D. to use: specific to general or general to specific. Choose the one that will help your readers understand and act upon the information you're giving them.

M.O.D. #6 is useful for: customer-service communications, letters of understanding, performance appraisals, proposals, training materials, work orders.

M.O.D. #7: Analysis

When you analyze a problem, you examine its component parts and learn about their relationships to one another and to the whole. Usually, your analysis is in response to a question that you've been asked. You answer that question by formulating hypotheses and rigorously testing them using the scientific method. You must be careful and thorough—not only as you conduct your analysis but also when you write it up.

There are two challenges to writing up your analysis:

1. How do you logically organize an analysis section?
2. How do you report your overall solution?

1. Trace your analytical process

Careful analysis is a complex task, yet you want your document to be easy to read and use. To achieve clarity, trace the process you followed step by step, and number each step. The parts of an analysis include:

1. Problem
2. Question
3. Hypotheses
4. Research
5. Solutions, which we like to call the "bottom line" (traditionally known as recommendations)

Conclusions are often paired with recommendations. If they are not the same, insert the conclusion before the solution. For example, your research shows that your company is growing so fast that you must move in six months (your conclusion). You suggest moving the company to Cleveland (your recommendation).

2. How do you report your solution? Put your bottom line on top

Don't confuse tracing your analytical process with presenting a recommendation based upon it. No matter what your sequence of discovery was, your bottom line (solution or recommendation) always goes near the beginning of your document. Most managers will not want to wade through your analytical process. Seriously consider putting it in the appendix unless you're sure your readers want it.

Imagine you're writing an evaluation for a venture capitalist, Chris Buck, who is trying to decide whether to invest in a biotech start-up company. You have a 75-page report documenting the viability of the new company. How should you analyze the report to help Chris decide? Examine each factor that contributed to the results of the study. Weigh each carefully—one or two factors are bound to emerge as significant.

Analytical development requires a sharp, detail-minded writer. You can't overlook a single aspect with this M.O.D.: business plan, products, people, research-and-development costs, the market, the competition—everything. You're searching for the critical factors that will mean success or failure.

For more help on writing a complex, research-based report, turn to "Report Credibly" in Part 3. If you are preparing a presentation that has an analytical component, consult Part 2: "Writing Presentation Documents™."

M.O.D. #7 is useful for: annual reports, audit reports, feasibility studies, lab reports, presentations, problem-solving memos and reports, strategic reports and plans, technical reports, trouble reports, yearly overviews.

Other factors in your choice of a M.O.D.

Your readers' needs are not the only criteria for choosing your method of development. You will discover that certain types of information just naturally lend themselves to a particular method. For example, how could you fail to choose a chronological M.O.D. for a report titled *From MiniTrix, Inc., 1999, to GigaTrix, Inc., 2019: How the Company Grew*?

As you can see, many of the M.O.D.s explained in this chapter are complementary. Sometimes you need more than one. Combine as many as necessary to create the structure that presents your material most clearly and persuasively. The following chart lists M.O.D.s that might be useful for specific document sections or even a single paragraph. Even in short documents, different sections may require different M.O.D.s.

Which M.O.D. Should You Use for a Document Section?

If you are writing…	Order of importance	Chronology	Process	Organization in space	Comparison/contrast	Specific to general/g. to s.	Analysis
Accident descriptions		✓					
Analyses		✓	✓		✓		✓
Customer-service responses	✓					✓	
Demographic studies				✓	✓		
Descriptions			✓	✓		✓	
Economic forecasts	✓						✓
Financial analyses	✓				✓		✓
Findings	✓						
Statistics	✓				✓		✓
Instructions	✓		✓	✓			
Procedures/processes		✓	✓	✓			
Research or test results	✓				✓		
Test protocols		✓	✓				
Work orders		✓	✓		✓		

Several parts of this book deal with the organizational problems of particularly long and complex documents. Are you writing a proposal or organizing a report? Consult Part 3. For presentations, see Part 2.

On your own: Read over some old reports written by you or your colleagues to see if you can detect what M.O.D.s they used. Label the different types in the margin. Was one method favored over others?

How do you organize your writing time?

By now you may be thinking, "If I do all the planning you're suggesting, it's going to take me *twice* as long to write, not half as long." Fortunately, this isn't true, and the proof is in the following chart.

Are You Organizing Your Writing Time the Way Professional Writers Do?

	You	Professional writer
Planning	_____%	50%
Drafting	_____%	20%
Editing	_____%	30%

Fill in the first column. To write a typical memo, what percentage of your time do you spend in each category? Now look at the second column. This is how professional writers allocate their time. If you follow our Six Steps, you too will find yourself dividing your time this way. The result? You'll join the ranks of the thousands of Better Communications graduates who say that they've cut one third off their writing time.

Step 5:
Write the First Draft

Now that you've clustered and sequenced your ideas, you are ready to write a quick-and-dirty first draft. The challenge is to write only—without editing. Don't let the critic in you compete with your creative self as you draft sentences! Wait until all your thoughts are on paper before polishing and refining your writing. Editing each sentence as you write it only breaks your concentration.

Content vs. form

After the planning stages, the writing task consists of two very different activities:

1. writing, or generating content—a creative process
2. editing, or structuring the form—an analytic process.

If you try to do both activities at the same time, you will lose speed. If in the middle of the first draft, for example, you stop for several minutes to grope for the perfect word, you'll no doubt grind to a halt. Leave a space where the word belongs and fill it in later. Try to keep up your speed as you did when free writing.

Start anywhere

Don't get hung up on that first, most difficult sentence. You can sit at your desk for hours worriedly rewriting your opener. If the first sentence is not immediately apparent, forget about it and get on with your writing. You can go back later, when the pressure is off, and write the perfect sentence. Some of the best beginnings are written last—after you have a full view of your document.

Headlines help you decide where to start

Review the headlines you created in Step 3 to decide which sections you'll tackle first. Maybe you're the type who prefers to get the easy material out of the way immediately. On the other hand, you may want to go after a difficult section first because you feel alert and up to the challenge. In short, start with whatever section appeals to you.

How to construct paragraphs

Before you launch into your first draft, it's worth reviewing paragraph construction. Paragraphs are the building blocks of any document. Their purpose is threefold:

- to develop the single idea presented in the topic sentence or headline
- to provide a logical break in material
- to create physical breaks that help the reader visually.

Well-constructed paragraphs have unity and coherence. *Unity* means focusing on one idea only. *Coherence* is linking sentences and ideas logically by using transitional words.

Stick to one idea for each paragraph (for unity)

When you ramble from idea to idea, you confuse your readers. Most readers prefer to handle one idea at a time. They count on paragraph breaks to signal the completion of one thought and the beginning of the next.

Begin with a topic sentence or headline. Since your readers usually want to get the point immediately, present a summary of your paragraph's main point early. The bottom-line-on-top principle applies to paragraphs, too. Here are some examples of topic sentences that capture your readers' attention:

> Capital spending declined drastically in April.
> The XYZ system will reduce overhead by 50 percent.
> Certificates of deposit provide safe, if low-yield, investment income.

The remainder of the paragraph builds on the thought expressed in the topic sentence, perhaps by answering "how" or "why."

Incorporate transitions and linkage (for coherence)

Transition words such as *therefore* and *however* are signposts that help your readers follow your logic and your flow of ideas. Be careful to choose the appropriate transition. The sentences that follow show how meaning changes with different transition words, and how unclear the point remains if no transitions are used.

> Jessica is compiling the research. I'll interview the client.
> Jessica is compiling the research. *Meanwhile,* I'll interview the client.
> Jessica is compiling the research. *However,* I'll interview the client.
> Jessica is compiling the research. *Therefore,* I'll interview the client.

Do your readers a favor: use transitions to link your ideas both between or within sentences and between paragraphs.

How to use transition words

Choose your transition words according to the relationship you want to establish between ideas. Here are some examples:

Contrast: however, although, but, conversely, nevertheless, yet, still, on the other hand
Comparison: similarly, likewise, in the same way
Cause and effect: as a result, therefore, consequently, thus, so, because
Example: for instance, for example, specifically, to illustrate
Addition: moreover, besides, in addition, also, too
Time: now, later, after, before, meanwhile, following, then
Sequence: first, second, third, next, last, finally (not first*ly,* second*ly*)

Use conjunctions between sentences—occasionally

The coordinating conjunctions—*and, but, yet, or, nor, for*—are used to connect ideas *within* sentences. They can also be used like the transition words listed previously—that is, to connect ideas *between* sentences. Traditional grammarians may object, but other writing experts say that occasional use of a coordinating conjunction to begin a sentence improves the flow and clarity of a paragraph. And we agree.

Carefully choose a coordinating conjunction to show *precisely* the relationship of ideas you intend. For example, use *and* only to show that the next idea is an addition to the previous idea. Don't use *and* merely to string ideas together.

Use reference words and repetition for linkage

Link your ideas by referring to or repeating the topic or key words. Use reference words like *this, that, these, those,* and other pronouns to tie in new ideas with points made earlier. Within and between paragraphs, linkage gives logical flow to your thoughts.

An easy way to improve clarity and flow

Here is an example of no linkage within a paragraph:

> Our Project Management Services Group provides targeted services throughout all project stages. Strategy and Development makes sure that marketing plans are aligned with overall business goals. Program Implementation assures follow-through with strategy decisions at all levels. Systems Integration tackles design and technology challenges, and Quality Assurance monitors progress throughout.

Rewriting these sentences using linkage and transition words improves both flow and clarity:

> Our Project Management Services Group provides targeted services throughout all project stages. *First,* Strategy and Development makes sure that marketing plans are aligned with overall business goals. *Then* Program Implementation assures follow-through with strategy decisions at all levels, *as* the Systems Integration group tackles design and technology challenges. *Throughout this process,* Quality Assurance monitors progress.

Now let's try adding transitions between paragraphs. How would you improve the following passage?

> Tom is an outstanding team player who has quickly won the respect of his colleagues. He is open to advice from his peers as he learns his new responsibilities; at the same time, he is eager to help newer members of the department when he can.
>
> Tom has exceeded the performance standard for customer service. Even when a customer has a complicated problem, Tom will persist until he has resolved it.
>
> Last month, one of our customers with an older system called in because he was having trouble running our software. Tom had to consult with our engineers several times, but he found a solution.

See how adding a few transition words improves overall flow:

> Tom is an outstanding team player who has quickly won the respect of his colleagues. He is open to advice from his peers as he learns his new responsibilities; at the same time, he is eager to help newer members of the department when he can.
>
> *In addition,* Tom has exceeded the performance standard for customer service. Even when a customer has a complicated problem, Tom will persist until he has resolved it.

For example, last month one of our customers with an older system called in because he was having trouble running our software. Tom had to consult with our engineers several times, but he found a solution.

Paragraphs are the building blocks

Now that we've reviewed how to write an effective paragraph and the uses of transitions and connectors, it's time to start writing.

Write your draft

Write down a headline, then write a paragraph

Without regard to style or grammar, write one paragraph for each headline. Be bold—put down your content, even if the sentences are messy and graceless. Resist your internal critic if it tries to derail your train of thought. You can clean up the draft later.

Add more headlines as subtopics emerge

Don't be surprised if you haven't thought in advance of every possible headline you'll need in your document. As you write, you'll no doubt discover many subtopics you want to mention. Simply add headlines or topic sentences as you need them—this is a predictable part of the process.

Use a subject line to begin memos, e-mail, and letters

A good subject or "Re:" line answers the reader's first question: "What's this all about?" Later, it helps the reader recall the contents at a glance. In a letter, place the subject line, in boldface type, two lines below the salutation. Some companies prefer to put the subject line between the inside address and the salutation.

In e-mail, put your bottom line in the subject line and include an action verb. For example:

Subject: Send survey results by 7/14, please

Think like an advertiser: don't miss a chance to reinforce your message. Use a date, not "today" or "tomorrow"—your recipient might not be in the office.

The myth of the perfect first draft

No matter what they say on the talk shows, very few professional writers produce a perfect draft the first time around. "But," you say, "I'm not a professional writer. I'm just trying to get through my daily workload. I simply don't have the time for several drafts."

But sending an imperfect, poorly worded first draft only creates more work in the long run, as you respond to your readers' questions with follow-up calls, e-mails—and rewrites of your first draft. Even e-mail, if it's at all sensitive or important, may require more than one draft. A team-writing project usually requires several.

People who believe it's possible to write a perfect draft the first time around probably think that's the most efficient way to write. Unfortunately, this misconception prevents them from maximizing their time. In fact, writers who aim to produce a perfect document with their first draft usually find themselves facing paralysis and confusion. This is because they are trying to do two very different things at once: write and edit.

To save time and minimize frustration, simply dive into this first draft with the aim of getting *something* on paper, rather than trying to get it perfect.

Efficiency tip: try writing with a time limit

One way to start your first draft is to write with a time limit. The ticking clock may prevent you from daydreaming. As in the free-writing Start-up Strategy you may have used in Step 2, fill a page as quickly as you can, but this time do not allow your thoughts to wander. Stick to the topics you've clustered under each headline. (If you find the time pressure bringing on writer's block, this strategy is not for you.)

On your own: The next time you are ready to start a draft, try this. Time yourself as you draft a page. Write your start time at the top of the page. Then, when you're finished, write your finish time at the bottom.

How long did it take you? If you filled the page in five minutes or less, you're doing well. If it took you longer than five minutes, or if you filled only half a page, you were probably worrying too much about word choice or sentence construction. It's the myth of the perfect first draft again! You should be able to write down several ideas quickly, even if they are roughly worded.

Try the exercise once more on another topic, and don't edit yourself as you go along.

Try dictating your first draft

Many seasoned writers find that the first draft flows more easily from their lips than from their fingertips. Those with experience estimate that they can dictate about six times faster than they can write. If you could increase your productivity by six times, wouldn't it be worth switching to this method? And if you are, or used to be, an experienced dictator, don't let your skills get rusty. They will be valuable once voice-recognition software is in everyday use.

When we covered dictating in Step 2, we explained how to move random, unorganized ideas from your brain onto the page. In Step 2 you rarely paused; but when you dictate your draft during Step 5, turn the machine off when you need a minute to regroup or formulate a thought.

To begin

With your sequenced Start-up Strategy or notes before you, begin drafting your document by speaking rather than writing. Even if you feel a little awkward at first, keep going.

Don't worry about perfection. Avoid editing or censoring yourself. For now, you just want to get the draft on tape; you can correct grammar and sentence structure once it's on paper.

Dictated drafts need careful editing

Avoid the common error of mailing out your unedited draft. Use dictating to get your paragraphs written, but always review the transcript carefully. Some good news: you've saved so much time by dictating that you'll come out ahead, even after editing.

Is it time to edit yet?

If you've managed to avoid editing yourself until now, you should feel proud. It's not easy to keep writing while your internal critic is giving you a running commentary on your every word. Before you begin to edit, there's one more step to help you shift gears.

Get distance

If you're too close to your work, it's hard to be objective about it. Getting distance means putting your writing away for a while so that you can come back to it with a fresh perspective. With enough time between writing and editing, it will be easier to approach your material as if someone else had written it. Other people's errors are always easier to spot than your own.

For example, you may think you wrote perfectly clear instructions for your assistant to purchase a new workstation. When you review your memo, you realize you forgot to specify the type of financing you wanted him to arrange—a potentially costly omission.

Another example is the following ad. Can you find the ambiguity?

Was the advertiser an employer who wanted to hire a copy editor, or an editor who was looking for a job? It's impossible to tell. The posting was a waste of both time and money. Even the shortest and simplest document, including e-mail, needs a moment of getting distance to prevent such errors.

How much time can you spare?

Of course, it's often difficult to allow yourself the luxury of getting distance with a schedule full of do-it-now deadlines. However, getting distance is *an integral part of the editing process.* If putting your writing away for a day or two is impossible, then try to complete your first draft just before you leave for the day. Even a lunch break or a ten-minute walk will help. You owe it to yourself and your reader to leave time between the writing and the editing.

Beating writer's block

Are you still finding it impossible to start despite following the Six-Step Process to the letter? Don't worry—everyone is hit with writer's block sooner or later. Try changing environments: find a quiet place to work, with no distractions. Or take a break. Leave your draft for a while: get up and stretch; walk around. Come back to the job refreshed.

When you get bogged down in one section of your draft, skip to another that you know you can write. If, after returning to the problem section, you still can't get past it, ask a coworker to take a look at what you have so far. Outside suggestions help.

Follow our advice, and before you know it, your draft will be done. Now it's time to switch gears, from the creative, writing part of the process to the more analytic job of editing.

Step 6:
Edit for Clarity, Conciseness, Accuracy, Visual Design, and Tone

Welcome back from your "getting distance" break. You've arrived at Step 6, and it's time to edit. From this vantage point, you will be able to revise so that your reader can understand you quickly and easily. This section focuses on the basics of editing—not grammar. For a grammar review, turn to Part 5.

Use the "*Be Your Own Editor*" Checklist

The "*Be Your Own Editor*" *Checklist* on pages 70–71 serves as an outline for this chapter. More important, use it from now on to make sure your documents are reader centered. The checklist will be your guide as you refine and polish the draft.

The "Be Your Own Editor" Checklist

☞ *Be sure to check these items for short documents.*

1. CONTENT

Purpose
- ☞ ❑ Clear to the reader?
- ☞ ❑ Specific in requests for actions or information?

Information
- ❑ Accurate and complete?
- ❑ Detailed enough?
- ❑ Persuasive in listing benefits to the reader(s)?

Personalize this checklist with your own writing issues

_____
_____
_____
_____
_____
_____
_____

2. SEQUENCE

Bottom Line
- ☞ ❑ At the top?
- ❑ If not, strategically placed?

Organization
- ❑ Logically presented?

3. DESIGN

Format
- ☞ ❑ Enough headlines, sidelines, and bulleted and numbered lists?
- ☞ ❑ White space to frame ideas?
- ☞ ❑ Highlighted deadlines and action items?

Presentation
- ❑ Most effective for statistical information?
- ❑ Would a chart, table, or graph be better?

4. STRUCTURE

Paragraphs
- ❑ Headlines worded for impact?
- ❑ Begin with a topic sentence?
- ❑ Focus on one topic?
- ❑ Use transitions to connect ideas?
- ☞ ❑ Stay within 5–6 lines in length?

Sentences
- ❑ Varied in structure and length?
- ☞ ❑ Streamlined to 15–20 words?

5. TONE AND STYLE

Words
- ❑ Simple, specific, and straightforward?

	❑ Free of affectation and gobbledygook?
	❑ Acronyms explained and terminology familiar to readers?
Style	❑ Personable, upbeat, and direct?
	❑ Appropriate for the audience?
	❑ Active voice?
	❑ Positive approach?
	❑ The "you" attitude?

6. FINAL PROOF

☞ ❑ Are grammar, punctuation, and spelling correct?

❑ Did you run the spell-check program?

❑ Should someone else review it?

❑ If this is a repeat mailing, did you highlight new information?

Now, let's look more closely at each phase of the editing process.

1. Content

Before you go any further, stop to review what you've done in Steps 1 and 2. There's no point in refining and polishing your draft until you're sure you've successfully analyzed your audience, defined your purpose in writing, and generated the right content.

Review Step 1: Analyze your audience and define your purpose

This review is essential if you are to do an effective editing job. By reviewing your analysis, you will have it fresh in your mind. Use this opportunity to refocus on your audience and purpose. If you discover you've changed your mind significantly about either, you may need to alter your work in Steps 1–4.

Review Step 2: Generate ideas

With your audience and purpose in mind, see if you have included the right kind as well as the right amount of information. Knowing exactly how much information to present isn't always easy. It takes as much skill to decide what to omit as what to include. Ask yourself:

- Do I have enough data to persuade my reader?
- Am I including too much?
- What is necessary and relevant for my audience and purpose?

It's not too late to add or delete content, but don't bombard your reader with unnecessary information just because you did the research.

2. Sequence

Review the organization of your document—how you grouped and sequenced information.

Review Step 3: Group information under headlines

With audience and purpose in mind, check the headlines you've written for each paragraph. Are they on target—specific rather than generic? Do they truly describe the contents of the paragraph?

Review Step 4: Sequence your ideas

Review the big-picture sequence of your sections. Have you chosen the best method(s) of development to suit both your audience and purpose? For example, are meeting minutes organized chronologically while emphasizing significant developments or decisions? Have you organized your report so that your readers don't have to wade through the process of discovery (as you did when you researched the report)?

This is your last chance to change the sequence of information. Is your bottom line on top? Or as close as possible?

Are you satisfied with what you've written so far?

If your answer is yes, then think about your document's visual impact. You're ready to proceed to the next step in the editing process: designing your document to best present your message.

If your answer is no, try the following technique.

The rewriting strategy

Sometimes your letter, e-mail, or paragraph just doesn't sound right. In this situation, it may be more efficient simply to put aside your draft and start again.

Words are not precious; there are plenty more where the first ones came from. The Nobel Prize–winning writer Isaac Bashevis Singer called the wastebasket "the writer's best friend." Today we might accord that honor to the delete key.

Rewriting can be as efficient as revising when you're stuck. Take the strategy seriously. For some frustrated managers, rewriting has dramatically changed their ability to get past the tough spots. Professional writers use it constantly. Try it enough times to give it a chance to work.

On your own: Quickly write a one-screen e-mail memo on any topic. After you've finished, save it and start again. Don't look at the first one. Repeat the process a third time. Now compare the three drafts. Chances are you'll prefer a later draft. Why?

Suggested topic: You recently interviewed a promising candidate for an important position in your department. You want to offer him the job, but you've heard he's about to take a position elsewhere. In a letter, offer him the position and try to convince him that this is his best choice.

3. Design

When a document is easy to read and key points seem to jump out at you, that document has visual impact. Clear writing alone is not enough. Take the time to create a visual design that *entices* readers. It will help your message stand out from the hundreds of documents that regularly bombard readers.

Put yourself in your readers' shoes

When you check through the material in your in-box, what makes you read one document instead of another? Without even realizing it, you probably choose documents that look appealing because they

- use headlines liberally
- keep paragraphs short
- include lists
- allow for plenty of white space
- underscore important steps or dates
- use a different typeface to make important information stand out.

Make your format work for you

Consciously or unconsciously, readers develop attitudes toward a piece of writing—and the writer—from the appearance of the writing alone. They make judgments about how difficult it is to read or how organized it may be. They also notice and appreciate the writer's effort to make a document visually appealing. Carefully designed documents tell your readers that you care not only about your message but also about them. Make your format work for you—not against you.

How to Create Visual Impact: a design checklist

Even the simplest formatting techniques make a big difference in the appearance and the readability of your document. Now that you've finished your draft, design your document with this checklist in mind. Use it to review all of your writing until it becomes second nature.

How to Create Visual Impact: A Design Checklist

You can use . . .	to . . .
Headlines	introduce most paragraphs
	focus your reader on your major ideas
Sidelines	add extra emphasis
	help persuade
Different fonts	assure readability
	unify style
Short paragraphs	avoid overwhelming your reader
	attract speed readers
Two columns	convey two kinds of information simultaneously
	encourage faster reading
Bulleted lists	replace lists within sentences
Numbered lists	indicate sequence
	list steps in a procedure
	provide easy reference to the list
	quantify items
White space and indentation	frame your ideas
	improve readability
Graphs, charts, and tables	present numbers and dollar amounts
	present technical data
Color (use judiciously)	highlight information (limit to two colors)
	add aesthetic appeal
Illustrations and photographs	depict or explain objects and their components
	make the abstract concrete
	add interest
Boldface or *italics*	emphasize deadlines and action items
Different fonts or sizes	
Borders, boxes, or shading	

Let's examine each of these design elements.

Use headlines for most paragraphs

As we discussed in Step 3, headlining means choosing a few words that illustrate the content of the paragraph, visually emphasizing them, and using them to introduce each paragraph. For more on headline editing, see "Reword Headlines for Impact" on p. 86. Here we'll deal with formatting.

Headline format

Follow these guidelines:

- Capitalize only the first word in most headlines, except for proper nouns.
- Boldface or italicize headlines to separate them clearly from the text. You may also use a contrasting font.
- Line up headlines flush left.
- Don't use punctuation after headlines, except for question marks and occasional exclamation points. Colons are unnecessary.

If you're writing a report or other document with many sections and subdivisions, design a hierarchy of different headline levels before you begin to write. The hierarchy should reflect the outline of the report, with headlines on the same level all following the same format. You can vary the following options:

- font style and size
- format: boldface, italics, all caps, small caps
- position on the page (such as flush with the left margin, centered, or indented)
- capitalization.

Make the task easy: use the headline styles built into your word-processing program. Or consult the *Instant-Answer Guide to Business Writing* by Deborah Dumaine for an example of a headline hierarchy.

Readers prefer headlined letters

Headlines are increasingly accepted in business-letter writing. Introducing memolike headlines may detract a bit from the personal quality of some letters, but they add clarity and efficiency.

Have you ever heard anyone complain about a well-designed document? We never have—we only hear about the ones that are poorly designed. More and more of our clients agree that letters, like reports and memos, need attention to visual presentation. A headlined letter presents information effectively.

Use sidelines for extra emphasis and persuasion

Like headlines and subject lines, sidelines attract readers' attention and may add to a document's persuasiveness. Sidelines are functionally the same as headlines; it's just that they are placed to the left side of the text. An example of sideline use in a proposal follows.

Tuition Reimbursement Proposal

Recommended action We recommend implementing a tuition-reimbursement program to ensure that Glitch Inc. can retain and support high-potential employees. Employees who have been employed at Glitch for at least two years will be able to take advantage of company-paid courses or degrees.

How this plan will further corporate goals

Controls costs A tuition-reimbursement proposal will control costs by decreasing employee turnover and, therefore, the cost of hiring. We will save time and money in the following areas:
- advertising
- screening and interviewing
- transportation and relocation costs
- new-employee orientation and ramp-up time.

Encourages motivation and productivity Today's educated and ambitious workers expect and value developmental and educational options. The new policy will encourage greater productivity by improving both the business and the professional skills of our people.

Improves recruitment and retention Other companies have experienced a decrease in turnover when they have added a tuition-reimbursement program. This policy will help Glitch meet and even exceed the competition in recruiting and retaining high-quality employees. Line managers, too, will benefit from increased access to new developmental tools.

Uses time efficiently The proposed policy will lighten the total administrative burden for the training staff, participants, and participants' managers by approving a degree program instead of each individual course.

The following excerpt from a user's manual shows how to format technical information using headlines and sidelines.

On-Line Table Handling: Internal and External Tables

A table can be internal to the programs that use it or can be kept external and loaded when needed.

A. How to access internal tables

The programs include an internal table used in one of two ways.

Use C++ copy statement	First, you can copy it into the program itself using a C++ copy statement. To test a new version of such tables requires a recompilation and relink edit of all the programs that use it.
Use link edit	Second, you can link-edit the table with a program. In this case, the C++ program calls the routine containing the table to pass it back to the calling program. A change to such a table causes a relink edit of all the programs that use it to include the new copy.
No overhead involved	Although a change to an internal table affects each program that uses it, accessing the table involves little or no overhead.

B. How to access external tables

Use assembler language routine	The C++ program accesses external tables by calling an assembler language routine that loads the table from an external library and passes it back to the calling program.

C. Working in a batch environment

Use previously loaded copy	In a batch environment, the first time the C++ program requests an external table, the table comes up from the available copy previously loaded. When the program terminates, IMS/VS automatically deletes the table.

Vary the fonts

Serifs, the small projections at the end of each stroke of a letter, improve readability. Use a serif font for body text; **for contrast, you may use sans serif (without serifs) for headlines.** Except for professionally designed documents, limit yourself to two fonts maximum. More than two looks cluttered—the exact opposite of the simplification you are striving for.

Keep paragraphs to 5–6 lines maximum

We'll discuss paragraph structure later in this chapter, in the "Edit Paragraphs" section. For now, note that paragraphs in single-column text on standard-sized paper should be limited to five or six lines.

Use multiple columns

The narrower the column, the faster people are able to read. If you use a two- or three-column format, busy people may well read more of your document.

If you are designing a document for both technical and nontechnical readers, try a two-column format that presents two versions of your document. One side is more technical and detailed for your technical audience; the other, briefly summarizing key issues and defining technical points, is directed toward managers and other nontechnical readers.

Bullet or number each item in a vertical list

Vertical lists emphasize your message far better than lists embedded in sentences. They attract the reader's attention and make a list easy to digest. Indent a vertical list and bullet or number each item. If your e-mail system doesn't have a bullet function or if you think your recipient's system won't hold the formatting, use hyphens instead.

Formatting a vertical list

Use a colon to introduce a list.

> Take the following safeguards to protect trade secrets:
> - limit public access to and within buildings
> - screen employees rigorously
> - conduct exit interviews
> - disclose information to employees on a "need-to-know" basis.

Omit the colon if the last word is a verb or preposition, or if each item finishes the sentence.

> Protect company trade secrets by
> - limiting public access to and within buildings
> - screening employees rigorously
> - conducting exit interviews
> - disclosing information to employees on a "need-to-know" basis.

If the list completes the introductory sentence, put a period after the last item only. Do not capitalize the items in the list. If the items are complete sentences, write them as such: capitalize the first word and put a period after each item.

Stay parallel

Parallel structure in a list means that all the items have the same grammatical form. Use single words, similar phrases, or similarly constructed sentences for each item. Begin each item with the same part of speech (verb, noun, adjective). The following list is not parallel.

Protect company trade secrets by
- limiting public access to and within buildings
- rigorous employee screening
- employee exit interviews
- disclosing information to employees on a "need-to-know" basis.

Now it is parallel:

Protect company trade secrets by
- *limiting* public access to and within buildings
- *screening* employees rigorously
- *conducting* exit interviews
- *disclosing* information to employees on a "need-to-know" basis.

For a review of parallelism, see pp. 219–221.

Bullets or numbers?

Use bullets for a list that doesn't have a specific order. Use numbers instead of bullets, however, if you want to show steps or sequence. Numbers are especially helpful in procedures, when you are explaining "how to." They provide a visual signal that tells the reader how to read the information and an easy reference mechanism for discussing documents with others, especially remotely.

Don't overuse bullets

Bullets list points but can't relate them to one another. Ideas that are only listed, not linked, may sound disjointed and illogical. An overbulleted document is just as tedious to read as a page of dense prose. When you need to show contrast or cause and effect, use a paragraph or a chart.

Frame your ideas with white space

White space is created by separation between paragraphs and sections. It also occurs between headlines and text and in the margins—top, bottom, left, and right. Use white space to give the reader a visual break and make your document look less dense. Moreover, white space surrounding text showcases important information.

Use indentation to highlight subordinated topics or lists

Indenting subtopics and lists will call your reader's attention to the big picture. Indent to send a visual signal to your reader that you are supporting a key idea with data that explain or expand it. The white space that indentation creates draws the reader's eye to the list and makes for easy reference later.

Be consistent: use the same indentation throughout your document for the same type of content. Don't indent one list a quarter of an inch, the next half an inch, and center the next in the middle of the page.

Put information in charts, graphs, and tables

Tables, charts, and graphs are excellent tools for displaying complex numeric data. They offer a welcome contrast to a solid block of text. Vary your charts to hold your reader's interest, and intersperse text with tables and charts instead of grouping them all together. Never use charts for decorative effect—your goal is to state your message clearly and concisely.

Use color judiciously

Color adds interest, but don't overuse it; it may distract your reader from key content. As always, consider who your audience is and what image you wish to convey. Use colors to highlight information, but limit yourself to two.

Will your readers make black-and-white copies of your color document for distribution? Check the impact of loss of color, especially on charts. Eliminating color can ruin a chart's message.

Include graphics and illustrations

Graphics create interest and provide variety. Use an illustration to replace several paragraphs of text, especially when describing objects such as new products or mechanisms. Like charts, illustrations should serve a purpose beyond the purely decorative.

Emphasize information to drive action

Boldface type calls attention to key action steps, dates, and deadlines. Use italics to highlight vital words, phrases, or ideas. You can also highlight with boxes, borders, and shading, either black and white or color. As with any visual technique, don't overdo emphasis; it will lose its impact.

Are you sending a revision or update?

Many times you learn just after sending a document that a detail has changed. Perhaps a deadline has been moved back or a product feature altered. Alert your readers to changes by

- sending a new memo or e-mail noting only the change, or
- updating your original communication and marking the change in bold, in a border, or with a different font.

One senior executive told us his biggest pet peeve was "having to reread the whole document to sleuth out what was different from the first version."

An example of good visual design

The letter on pp. 82–83 combines many of the design elements we've just discussed:

- headlines that give a quick overview of paragraph content
- sidelines for extra emphasis
- font variety between headline and paragraph text to add visual interest
- short paragraphs and white space to improve readability
- bulleted lists to emphasize information
- a chart that makes numeric data easy to read and provides a break from text.

International, Inc.

88 International St.   Secaucus, NJ 07666   E-mail: info@intlinc.com   T: 201.555.1863

November 20, 2009

Ms. Gabrielle Valmont, Manager
Amalgamated Chemicals, Inc.
Four Amalgamated Place
Ottawa, Ontario A1B 2C3

Dear Gabrielle:

Subject: Finalizing our joint venture for Project Phoenix
To meet the future requirements for our companies' joint effort, Project Phoenix, I am putting together the International, Inc., negotiating team that will work with Amalgamated Chemicals, Inc. The team will need to discuss our immediate and long-term needs.

IMMEDIATE NEED
A proposal by December 20
For our team to assess overall project feasibility and future requirements, I need your price proposal in writing by December 20, 2009. Our three-year product-requirement projections follow. Please bid on the following quantities of 12 mil 5/5 poly.

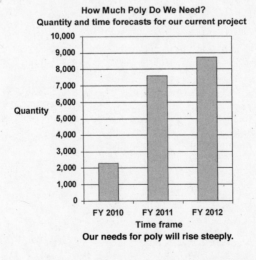

LONG-TERM NEEDS
Joint long-term goals

Partnership   Project Phoenix will contribute to our joint goal of becoming better partners. International will share its forecasts for total product needed during the next three years. Amalgamated, in turn, will help by giving International a discount on volume purchases.

Future projects   With successful completion of this joint project, we will have a proven format for future ventures, giving Amalgamated
- a complete picture of each project
- a competitive edge over other vendors.

Joint benefits

Since you will receive a three-year forecast for project requirements, you will be able to plan future labor and raw-material needs more efficiently. We will receive a price break for total requirements on each subproject, so we will be able to lower our bottom-line costs and become more competitive.

Partnering for alliances

Even beyond product forecasts, our largest partners expect us to explore fully with them issues critical to their success. Our alliance with you might also benefit from exploring these issues, which include

- just-in-time delivery
- longer amortization and capitalization periods
- electronic data interface
- representation at our weekly quality meetings and monthly staff sessions.

Additional action requested: set a meeting

Please call me to schedule a teamwide meeting that includes marketing and shop-floor personnel from both our organizations. You can reach me at 201.555.1863, ext. 33.

Gabrielle, you are an outstanding resource for us on this critical project. I'm looking forward to building a strong, mutually profitable relationship with you.

Sincerely,

Sam King

Sam King
Purchasing Specialist

On your own: Your manager has just handed you this report draft. The topic is "Third Quarter Sales Recap." He tells you, "I need to distribute this information at tomorrow's meeting. Please redo it and return it to me."

How would you design this document for visual impact?

This report analyzes our third-quarter results to see if our new training and referral programs have helped us to meet our goals. In addition, it determines how we can ensure our growth in the future.

So far, every quarter this year has been more profitable than the corresponding quarter of last year. Overall, it was our best quarter in three years, despite the sluggish economy. In particular, of the four offices in our district, our office had the highest percentage increase in sales revenues. In the first quarter, our revenues totaled $270 million and in the second quarter we increased to $300 million. However, in the third quarter, our revenues were up by 50 percent with $450 million in sales! In addition, last quarter, our office outperformed the company's other three offices. In fact, we accounted for 43 percent of the company's total revenues (the West team accounted for 23 percent; the South team, 18 percent; and the North team, 16 percent). This is a sizable increase from last year's standing when our office ranked as third most productive in the company.

We can maintain our success if our sales team takes action in a few main areas. First, they need to keep building relationships with our key clients through webinars. Then they need to continue our referral incentive program. Finally, they must deepen our company's knowledge and use of Client Relationship Manager (CRM) software.

Our current success can be attributed to several factors. We had several key clients give us more work than usual. The referral incentive program accounted for 27 percent of our new sales. In addition, the new CRM system we installed in the second quarter saved us millions of dollars in I.T. costs. Partly because of the new training program we started at the beginning of the year, each person in the sales group developed a targeted sales plan and exceeded his or her individual goal. Therefore, we were able to hire some additional people to our sales force. The entire sales group has now completed that training.

In summary, we've had a large increase in sales since the new programs began at the start of 2020, mostly due to our new training and referral programs. Our office is now the most productive in the company, compared with third most productive from last year. We'll continue to supervise these programs, and we expect a prosperous fourth quarter.

A companywide webinar has been scheduled for next week. The CEO has asked our team to share some of our success strategies. If you would like to share how you personally implemented one of our strategies, please see a partner.

Here are some possible solutions for communicating the message your manager wrote. You probably came up with others—a different type of chart, perhaps, or a table. Whatever your solution, note how a visual design that incorporates headlines, lists, and illustrations makes your document lively, interesting—and easy to read.

Q3 Sales Results and Strategy Evaluation
We met our goals and more!

The purpose of this report is to review and analyze our third-quarter results to determine
- if the new training and referral programs are helping us meet our goals
- how we can ensure future growth.

Q3 recap: Great news

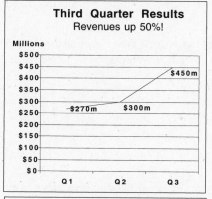

2020 has been a fantastic year, with each quarter more profitable than the corresponding quarter of last year. In fact, revenues were up 50 percent despite the sluggish economy. The third quarter was our best in three years.

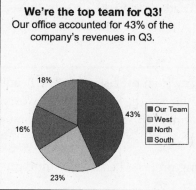

I am happy to report that we have even more to celebrate. Last quarter, our office was the top performing of the company's four offices. Last year at this time, we were third.

Recommendations: How we can maintain our success
Recommendations for continued success include the following actions for our sales team:
1. Keep building relationships with your key clients via webinars.

2. Continue our referral incentive program.
3. Deepen our knowledge and use of Client Relationship Management software.

How we met our goals

Our success can be attributed to a few key factors:
1. The new sales-training program helped all team members develop targeted sales plans.
2. Excellent service prompted key clients to request more work.
3. The referral incentive program generated 27 percent of our new sales.
4. We were able to hire additional salespeople.
5. Our new CRM system cut I.T. costs.

Summary: The new training and referral programs put us over the top

Since the new programs began at the start of 2020, we've had a dramatic increase in sales and our office has progressed from third most productive to most productive. We will continue to monitor these programs, and we expect a prosperous fourth quarter.

Next steps: Care to share?

The CEO has asked our team to share a few of our success stories during the upcoming companywide webinar. If you would like to share how you personally implemented one of our strategies, please see a partner.

4. Structure

If you are satisfied with your visual design, then you are finished formatting your draft. Now it's time to take a look at the wording of your headlines and the structure of your paragraphs and sentences. We'll begin with headlines. Are they as reader-centered as possible?

Reword headlines for impact

If the headlines in your draft were drawn primarily from the list of generic headlines in Step 3, then they may lack enough interest to engage the reader. Don't worry. Great headlines are a rare achievement during the drafting step. Now that your content is finalized, take a moment to give your headlines some impact.

Like other aspects of the Reader-Centered Writing process, headline writing gets easier with practice.

How to catch the reader's attention

First, scan your headlines. Do they flow in a logical sequence? Do they lead readers in the direction you want? Good headlines provide the reader with a quick overview of the document's major issues and follow a strategic method of development.

Next, ask yourself these questions:

1. Are my headlines specific and accurate?
2. Do they direct readers to my key points?
3. Is action emphasized?
4. Are they worded positively? Are they direct, yet polite?
5. Do they reach out to my readers?
6. Do action items and deadlines stand out? Our coaches say, "Deadlines require headlines!"

If your headlines could be better, here are some remedies for refining them to achieve maximum effect.

From boring to bold

Write a better headline without missing your deadline. Take one of these extra-strength remedies:

Remedy #1: Be specific. Replace a too broad and boring headline with a more concrete term—or combine the two.

> *Boring:* **Background**
>
> *Better:* **Our role in the wireless revolution**

> *Boring:* **Rationale**
>
> *Better:* **Rationale: to avoid potential liability**

Remedy #2: Include your point. This is B.L.O.T. (bottom line on top) at its best!

> *Boring:* **Recommendations**
>
> *Better:* **Recommendation: improve employee development**

> *Boring:* **Overview of our acquisition policy**
>
> *Better:* **How acquisitions have improved our balance sheet**

Remedy #3: Emphasize action. Highlight action by using active verbs.

> *Boring:* **Step 1**
>
> *Better:* **Getting started: reach for that *Focus Sheet***

Boring: **Last step**

Better: **Be your own editor and wrap it up right**

Boring: **Implementation**

Better: **Action recommended: test lab methodology in a pilot project**

Boring: **Background**

Better: **Why Cliptronics conducted an absenteeism study**

What started it all

How employee involvement jump-started this project

Remedy #4: Be positive. Good news attracts *and* persuades.

Negative: **Problem: absenteeism in the workplace**

Better: **Opportunity: increase productivity by reducing absenteeism**

Remedy #5: Ask questions. You'll find that questions

- combine the best of the above techniques
- are often part of your Start-up Strategy
- appeal to your *readers'* issues.

Boring: **R.O.I.**

Better: **What will be our Return on Investment (R.O.I.)?**

Boring: **Meeting agenda**

Better: **What should we accomplish in this meeting?**

Boring: **Ordering procedure**

Better: **How can you take advantage of this special price?**

Boring: **Timetable**

Better: **When can you expect the results?**

Remedy #6: Remember the Headlines Hall of Fame. Use these favorite headlines regularly:

Action requested	**Next steps**
Action recommended	**Deadline**
Action required	**Action taken**
Person to contact	**How to . . .**

A few final tips from our coaches

1. Brainstorm for words, phrases, or questions that best pinpoint your topic.
2. Try to give more information, rather than less.
3. Be sure to use the active voice.
4. Use a verb whenever you can. "Hire a Staff Accountant" is better than "Staff Accountant."

How creative can I be with my headlines?

Base your decision on an analysis of your audience and the tone you want to create.

"Where there's smoke there's *ire*" was the headline used by someone calling for a no-smoking policy outside the front door of a day-care center. It worked. But it might not work if smokers and nonsmokers have been at war with one another for years. "How secondhand smoke affects children's health" might be a better choice in that case.

Edit paragraphs

Once you're satisfied that your headlines have maximum impact, your next editing challenge is to revise the building blocks of the document—your paragraphs. Do they each contain just one idea? Are they short and well constructed? Did you use enough transitions and linkage to make good sense and smooth reading?

Paragraph length

Begin by scanning your paragraphs. Make sure that they're short. Long paragraphs look difficult to read, so find a place to break them up. Short paragraphs also keep the attention of speed readers. They often read only the first line of every paragraph, so the more paragraphs you have, the more they'll read.

An occasional one-sentence paragraph can be emphatic when you want a single idea to jump out at the reader, but a two-, three-, or four-sentence paragraph is the norm. Most often, you will need several subideas to explain or expand the key topic. In any case, it's not just the paragraph length that has visual impact—it's the white space created between paragraphs that makes for easy reading.

Paragraph structure

Your bottom line should be in the first or second paragraph unless you have deliberately chosen to put it elsewhere. Next, ask yourself these questions:

1. Does each paragraph focus on one idea only?
2. Does each paragraph begin with a topic sentence or a headline that serves the same purpose? If not, review "Stick to One Idea for Each Paragraph (for Unity)" on p. 60.
3. Do the paragraphs flow logically from one to the other?
4. Are the ideas within the paragraphs linked with transitions so that their relationships are clear? If not, review "Incorporate Transitions and Linkage (for Coherence)" on p. 61.

Reader-centered paragraphs get results

Revising your paragraphs won't take long if you follow the guidelines just described. The benefit to you is tremendous: you'll increase the chances that your document will be read—and acted upon.

Revise sentences

Now you're ready to refine and polish sentences. Put yourself in your readers' shoes as you reread. Use the following techniques to make each sentence straightforward, clear, and direct.

Streamline

Streamlining means weeding out any words or phrases that do not contribute to the readers' understanding. You can eliminate some words or phrases entirely, or eliminate one in a series of redundant words. For example, replace *at this point in time* with *now*. Or drop *again* from *resume again*. Get rid of the clutter. Hemingway said, "Writing is architecture, not interior decoration." This goes for business writing, too.

Streamlining also means rearranging or dividing sentences. Don't try to put too many ideas in a single sentence—one or two ideas will suffice. Two short and straightforward sentences are easier to read and understand than one long and complicated one.

Guideline: In general, sentences should be no more than 15 to 20 words each. Longer sentences are more difficult to read. They often slow readers down and may even put them to sleep! Sentence length should, however, be varied. A pileup of too many very short sentences will make your writing sound choppy or childish.

Suggestions for streamlining sentences:

- Don't use several words where one will do.
- Don't repeat yourself.
- Use the active voice. (See the following discussion under "Activate.")
- Use prepositional phrases sparingly.
- Break long sentences into shorter ones.
- Avoid *is where* and *is when.*
- Limit your use of *and* between phrases or clauses.

Here are some sentences before and after streamlining:

Before: At this point in time, we have not yet decided which action plan we will put into operation.

Revised: We have not yet chosen an action plan.

Before: In the event of an unexpected accident and you are a witness who saw the accident, you should file a completed accident report with the office of the safety director.

Revised: If you witness an accident, file an accident report with the safety director.

Before: Managers who are effective give praise to their employees who are outstanding workers and endeavor to implement motivational strategies with subordinates working under them who do not perform well.

Revised: Successful managers praise outstanding employees and try to motivate poor performers.

 On your own: To test your skill in streamlining sentences, try the exercise on p. 237.

Activate

Make your sentences come alive by using the active voice. Business writers unconsciously overuse the passive voice in sentences like this one: "New procedures are being documented this month." We are left to guess who is responsible for documenting. The active version is more straightforward and informative: "The I.T. process team is documenting the new procedures this month."

Writing in the passive voice, as the word implies, makes you sound aimless and ineffectual. It implies an unwillingness to take responsibility for your actions or assign responsibility to others. Don't hide behind statements like "Receipt of your letter is acknowledged." Instead, say, "We received your letter" or even "Thank you for your letter." So often we fail to give credit where it is due: "An excellent job was done." By whom?

Need a review?

Although grammatically correct, the passive voice is wordy and indirect. Readers prefer active sentences—they keep your tone lively and personable. Let's go over identifying the passive voice and changing it to active.

How to recognize active and passive sentences: In active sentences, the subject performs the action:

> The manager wrote the report.

In case you need a refresher, the *subject* of a sentence is what the sentence is about, or its topic. A subject can be a person, place, thing, or idea, and often it's the first important word in the sentence. *Verbs* are words expressing action or a state of being.

In passive sentences, something happens to the subject. The subject does not perform the action. In fact, many passive sentences don't mention who did the action:

> The report was written last week. (We don't know who wrote it.)
> Pat was authorized to write the report. (The subject, *Pat,* received the authorization but did not do the authorizing.)

Even though the following sentence tells us who did the writing, *manager* is not the subject:

> The report was written by the manager.

Passive sentences always contain some form of *to be* as a helping verb. A helping verb usually precedes the verb that expresses the action.

Subject (is acted upon)	To be helping verb	
1. The lab	is	inspected daily by John.
2. Research	was	done on the case.
3. Statements	were being	reconciled.

4. Susan	will be	oriented on Friday.
5. The checks	have been	sent.
6. Help	has been	provided to the homeless by XYZ, Inc.
7. I	am	not authorized by the president to approve the checks.

Here's a tip: Look for the word *by* with a name or title near the end of the sentence, as in sentences 1 and 6 preceding. If there is no *by* phrase, try adding "by George." If the sentence still makes sense, it is probably passive. For example, consider this sentence: "The meeting was called [by George]." This sentence is passive because you can add "by George." On which of the preceding sentences would this technique work?

In summary

You've spotted a passive sentence if

- the sentence uses a form of *to be* as a helping verb, and
- the subject is not performing the action the verb describes.

How to activate passive sentences

Once you've identified a passive sentence, change the word order to follow this pattern:

	Who does what?		
Passive:	The product was developed by Tech, Inc.		

	Who	**does**	**what?**
Active:	Tech, Inc.	developed	the product.

If a passive sentence doesn't supply the "who," you will have to provide it yourself.

Passive:	The contract will be awarded next week.		

	Who	**does**	**what?**
Active:	Our company	will award	the contract next week.

Voice and tense

Don't confuse passive voice with past tense. Both active and passive sentences can be in any tense. Here are examples of both active and passive sentences written in past, present, and future tense.

	Active	Passive
Past:	Payroll has sent the checks.	The checks have been sent.
Present:	Payroll is sending the checks.	The checks are being sent.
Future:	Payroll will send the checks.	The checks will be sent.

On your own: Try activating the preceding sentences 1–7 using this process. You'll come up with results like these active sentences:

Subject (performs action)	Active verb	
1. John	inspects	the lab daily.
2. Our department	did	the research on the case.
3. The accountant	reconciled	the statements.
4. Victor	will orient	Susan on Friday.
5. Payroll	has sent	the checks.
6. XYZ, Inc.	provides	help to the homeless.
7. The president	has not authorized	me to approve the checks.

The passive has its place

Deliberately choosing a passive over an active sentence is a question of strategy. If you do not know, or if it doesn't matter, who performed the action, use the passive voice:

> The system was shut down before the data were transferred.

Sometimes it's easier, safer, or more tactful not to say who performed the action in a sentence. The passive voice allows us to express our ideas without naming and blaming anyone:

> The report was not completed on time. (Your colleague did not complete the report, but you don't want to embarrass her on paper.)

If the passive voice is useful, why do we discourage it?

Businesspeople frequently overuse the passive because they think it's more professional. It certainly sounds more impersonal, but that isn't always desirable; for example: "It is expected that your promotion will be approved." This sentence is needlessly cold and awkward.

Use the active voice 90 percent of the time

Use the passive when it isn't necessary or desirable to say "who does what" or when you want to distance yourself from the message. Otherwise, use the active voice. The grammar-check function of your word-processing program will not only identify the passive voice, it will also tell you what percentage of your sentences are passive.

On your own: To test your skill in activating sentences, try the active-voice exercise on p. 239.

Now that you've edited your sentences, you can look more closely at the words themselves. Proceed to the next issue in the editing process: word choice.

Check words

Eliminate gobbledygook

Gobbledygook is stuffy, pompous language. As George Orwell said, "Never use a long word when a short one will do." Long words don't impress readers, and they confuse less educated ones. Jargon (the special vocabulary of a technical field) and coined words like *reincentivize* cloud meaning and slow readers down.

Using gobbledygook can make you sound insecure rather than professional—something no manager can afford. The following example illustrates the difference between gobbledygook and clear English.

> *Gobbledygook:*   We request that you endeavor to locate the communication inasmuch as the vice president regards it to be of great importance for next week's conference.
>
> *Better:*   Please try to find the letter because the vice president needs it for next week's conference.

Look for gobbledygook in every draft. Use the simplest possible language to express your ideas—readers will appreciate your straightforward style.

On your own: For practice eliminating gobbledygook from your writing, try the exercise on p. 241.

Tautologies: don't repeat yourself again

When you use a tautology, you're repeating yourself unnecessarily. Watch out for the following redundancies:

advanced ahead	important essentials	surrounding circumstances
attached hereto	just exactly	reduce down
at this point in time	merge together	resume again
basic fundamentals	mutual cooperation	round in shape
brief in duration	necessary requisite	seems apparent
both together	plan in advance	still continue
cooperate together	protrude out	true facts
enclosed herein	in the same way as described	young juveniles
final ending	hopeful optimism	2 A.M. in the morning

Eliminate sexist language

Traditionally, the pronoun *his* has been used to refer to men and women alike. Consider a sentence like this: "Every employee should turn in his work." Let's be realistic: using this sentence will raise eyebrows today. Resorting to traditional grammar rules to defend the use of *his* won't get you off the hook.

He/she doesn't solve the problem

To meet the need to refer to women directly, writers created *he/she* and *his/hers* or awkwardly referred to both *him and her*. Rather than resorting to these cumbersome usages, avoid them by rewriting your sentence. Where possible, use plural pronouns instead of singular ones.

Notice how plural pronouns let you use the neutral *their,* while singular pronouns force you to choose between *his* and *her.*

Plural subjects	. . . require . . .	plural pronouns.
Employees	should submit	their work.
People	should submit	their work.
All architects	should submit	their work.

Singular subjects	. . . require . . .	singular pronouns.
Each employee	should submit	his or her work.
Everyone	should submit	his or her work.

Sometimes it's too cumbersome or awkward to change to the plural, or this strategy just doesn't work in the given context. In such cases the solution is to alternate between "he" and "she." Say, for example, "The first question to ask when a successful executive departs is: Why is she leaving?" The next time you discuss the successful executive, use "he."

Wash that *-man* right out of your hair

Even though the suffix *-man* traditionally includes women, writers have invented words like *chairperson* (or simply *chair*) and *salesperson.* You don't, however, want to sound awkward or downright silly in your attempt to avoid sexist language. Rather than replacing *workmanship* with *workpersonship* or *manhole* with *personhole,* select a synonym or a descriptive phrase instead. Try *quality* for *workmanship.* As for *manhole,* you're on your own.

Be specific

One day Tom LeBlanc was working on a report describing market response to his company's recently developed system, the SLXQ. He had discussed the trends, growth indicators, and general market response. Using sentences like the following, he tried to explain why sales were not as high as predicted:

> The SLXQ has not met with the high degree of public acceptance predicted. Many customers seem to find the equipment too intimidating or cumbersome to learn to operate.

While this is useful information, it is very general and abstract. It needs to be followed with actual examples in order to come alive. To maintain reader interest and to clarify his point, Tom should include a real-life example—perhaps the story of Mr. Z, in Winnipeg, and the exact difficulties he encountered trying to operate the SLXQ.

Anecdotes, examples, and facts illustrate your abstract ideas, making them come alive. Without examples, your writing will seem dry or overly intellectual. Another problem with excessively vague or abstract writing is that it can be easily misinterpreted. Consider this sentence:

> The atmosphere in the conference room contributed to the outcome of the meeting.

Does it mean:

> The hostility among the committee members in the conference room contributed to the rejection of the proposal.

Or does it mean:

> The supportive atmosphere in the conference room contributed to meeting productivity.

Whenever possible, choose concrete words to express your ideas. Abstract writing is open to many interpretations, all potentially inaccurate. Therefore, make a real effort to clarify your ideas so that the reader understands your intention. Give examples and add words that create a picture in the reader's mind. Words that relate to the senses—sight, sound, touch, and smell—evoke the strongest response.

Here are a few examples of vague or abstract sentences followed by more concrete versions. Notice how much more helpful the second sentence is.

Abstract: The unit is malfunctioning.
Concrete: The freezer isn't making ice cubes.

Abstract: He amassed major input to determine the functional requirements for console construction.
Concrete: He interviewed many experts to learn how to build the console.

Abstract: If a situation like this occurs in the future, please involve others in the office before taking action.
Concrete: If you ever find the office door unlocked again, please ask people about it before calling in the FBI.

Abstract: Due to extenuating circumstances, we will have to delay introduction of our new product line for a while.
Concrete: We've decided to delay introduction of our new product line for six months while we iron out a wrinkle in the propulsion system. (For internal communications; not for customers.)

Lower the abstraction level in technical writing

The technical writers we meet are challenged by having to explain information unfamiliar to their readers. Yet they are the greatest offenders when it comes to being abstract.

Some writers in the technical world feel that giving examples and making creative comparisons is unprofessional. It's not. Real professionals help the reader any way they can. When trying to explain an abstraction like aerodynamics, a good writer will use a comparison as basic as the wings of birds.

Abstract obfuscation exercise

The passage that follows is too abstract—it needs some concrete examples. Put an X between any sentences where an example would help:

> When designing a Web site, make it easy for your users to navigate. It won't matter to your users how good your content is if they can't find what they need. Label your links and place them in predictable spots. In addition, beware of long, scrolling navigation pages. Use discretion with your color scheme. Also, your text should always be large enough for people to read. Any graphics you include should have an obvious purpose. Don't use technology features just because you can. Do not launch audio or video automatically.

Take a look at the same passage on p. 100, this time with examples inserted. Aren't you surprised at how much difference the examples make?

Notice how the addition of examples enhanced your understanding of the original passage. Suddenly, the piece came to life. Be watchful for places in your own writing where an example would reach out to your readers and add to their understanding.

5. Tone and style

How do you sound on paper—for example, serious, critical, or warm? Like tone of voice, the tone and style of your writing should be appropriate to your particular reader and the subject matter.

Choose the appropriate tone

Reviewing your *Focus Sheet* will help you reach out to your readers and determine the tone to adopt. Choose your words to fit your reader's personality and background. The best communicators adjust the way they write—and speak—depending on their audience. Think of the medical profession, for example. Some doctors do a wonderful job of making difficult medical issues comprehensible to their patients, without jargon or condescension. But you have probably met one or two who don't!

Good navigation is key to your Web site

When designing a Web site, make it easy for your users to navigate. It won't matter to your users how good your content is if they can't find what they need. Don't rely on the "Back" button as your primary navigation. Label your links and place them in predictable spots. Users are less likely to click an unlabeled URL, especially if it's long and complicated like this one: *http://pv2fd.pav2.melt.drd.com/cgibin/?curmbox=F00001%a=4ceda14563cd.*

Most users expect a link to a site's home page in the upper left corner of each page as well as links to your major pages at the bottom of each page. In addition, beware of long, scrolling navigation pages. Users tend to scan or select only the options that are immediately visible. Even those users who do scroll may get bored if the scrolling page is too long. Try not to make users scroll more than three to five screens.

Your text should be easy to read

Use discretion with your color scheme. Avoid overwhelming your text with too many bright or clashing colors. Choose background colors that contrast with your text so that it's easy to read. For example, use dark text on a light background. If you use a picture as your background, it might be hard to read text unless the picture is in muted colors. Also, text should always be large enough for people to read. Anything smaller than the equivalent of 10-point on paper is probably too small. Don't assume that your users know how to resize Web site text.

Graphics should enhance, not clutter, your message

Any graphics you include should have an obvious purpose. In particular, most people do not have the patience to sit through a graphics intro before entering your real site. Flashy graphics can slow your site's loading time, which could irritate your users. For all graphics you use, compress the file size as small as possible without sacrificing quality.

Avoid too many bells and whistles

Don't use technology features just because you can. For example, animations that run constantly are distracting. You may think flashing text or banners will catch your users' eye, but often they look so much like advertisements that users ignore them altogether. Do not launch audio or video automatically. You don't know where users are viewing the site or whether their systems can easily handle the files. Your users will appreciate having the choice.

Just as you may change the way you talk depending on the person you're with, why not do the same in your writing? Compare the tone of these two report titles:

Benefits of Acquiring the XLC System at Business, Inc.
How the Purchase of the XLC System Would Save Time, Money, and
Energy at Business, Inc.

In the first example, the tone is remote and abstract. The tone of the second title is more lively and persuasive, reflecting an awareness that the reader is one of the decision makers on the issue.

When you have a choice, be friendly and informal

Business writing continues to change in the direction of informality and straightforwardness. The friendlier and more "real" you sound, the better chance you have of relating to your reader. Be formal only when you feel it's the best way to reach your reader. Avoid stuffy sentences like "Should you require further assistance, please do not hesitate to write to my attention."

The following list shows some contemporary alternatives to the worn-out words and phrases that sound so pretentious today:

Instead of:	Use:	Instead of:	Use:
nevertheless	but	despite the fact that	although,
terminate	end		though
utilize	use	in view of the fact that	because,
deem	think		since
assistance	help	in order to	to
converse	talk	subsequent to	after
forward	send, mail	with reference to	about
advise	tell	on the occasion of	when
indicate	show	during the course of	during
reside	live	along the lines of	like
we would like to ask that	please	succeed in making	make
for the reason that	because	make use of	use
are of the opinion	believe	have need for	need
for the purpose of	for, to	give consideration to	consider
prior to	before	initiate, commence	begin, start

Detecting excessive formality in letters

There are many things wrong with the following letter, but the biggest problem is its extreme formality. Circle all the words or phrases that should be changed or eliminated to improve the tone.

January 23, 2020
Richard McKinney
Fogg Smoke Warning Systems
773 South Rodeo Drive
Los Angeles, CA 90000

Dear Mr. McKinney:

I wish to thank you for your prompt reply to my urgent telephone message of last week depicting the grave situation at hand. As you are no doubt aware, it is an absolute necessity for the safety of our patients and our entire staff to have an extensive and dependable smoke-warning system. Because of the unavailability of your customary repairman, Mr. Al Besto, we are compelled to hire a nonwarranted service firm. To be sure, an ounce of prevention is worth a pound of cure.

As you requested, I am forwarding a list of the rooms where the breakdowns occur most frequently. I am also enclosing a copy of the hospital floor plan, upon which I have noted the areas experiencing different types of breakdowns. Note: In some rooms (circled in red) the alarms ring at 20-minute intervals, certainly not conducive to the healing atmosphere of a hospital.

Also, another problem has arisen since we last corresponded. On several smoke detectors, the flashing light that is supposed to accompany the alarm lights up independently from said alarm. This has had particularly distressing consequences in Ward E, where countless patients have complained about flashing lights disturbing them late at night. It is expected that you will find this situation as intolerable as we do. At this point in time, no other flaws appear to exist.

Lastly, with respect to the warranty. Clearly, we cannot wait for Mr. Besto to repair the smoke-warning system, since he is hopelessly busy. Although I am cognizant that the Fogg policy normally covers expenses only when the repair work is done by our dealer—i.e., Mr. Besto—I presume that the policy will be relaxed in this disturbing circumstance, allowing us to engage an alternative firm. Would you be so kind as to make confirmation of this in writing?

I trust that you will contact me pursuant to these pressing issues at your earliest convenience. Your assistance is greatly appreciated.

Very truly yours,

Hiram Frost

Hiram Frost
Vice President, Physical Plant Safety

How did you do?

Compare your responses with the following. Did you pick out most of the problem areas?

January 23, 2020
Richard McKinney
Fogg Smoke Warning Systems
773 South Rodeo Drive
Los Angeles, CA 90000

Dear Mr. McKinney:

I wish to thank you for your prompt reply to my urgent telephone message of last week depicting the grave situation at hand. As you are no doubt aware, it is an absolute necessity for the safety of our patients and our entire staff to have an extensive and dependable smoke-warning system. Because of the unavailability of your customary repairman, Mr. Al Besto, we are compelled to hire a nonwarranted service firm. To be sure, an ounce of prevention is worth a pound of cure.

As you requested, I am forwarding a list of the rooms where the breakdowns occur most frequently. I am also enclosing a copy of the hospital floor plan, upon which I have noted the areas experiencing different types of breakdowns. Note: In some rooms (circled in red) the alarms ring at 20-minute intervals, certainly not conducive to the healing atmosphere of a hospital.

Also, another problem has arisen since we last corresponded. On several smoke detectors, the flashing light that is supposed to accompany the alarm lights up independently from said alarm. This has had particularly distressing consequences in Ward E, where countless patients have complained about flashing lights disturbing them late at night. It is expected that you will find this situation as intolerable as we do. At this point in time, no other flaws appear to exist.

Lastly, with respect to the warranty. Clearly, we cannot wait for Mr. Besto to repair the smoke-warning system, since he is hopelessly busy. Although I am cognizant that the Fogg policy normally covers expenses only when the repair work is done by our dealer—i.e., Mr. Besto—I presume that the policy will be relaxed in this disturbing circumstance, allowing us to engage an alternative firm. Would you be so kind as to make confirmation of this in writing?

I trust that you will contact me pursuant to these pressing issues at your earliest convenience. Your assistance is greatly appreciated.

Very truly yours,

Hiram Frost

Hiram Frost
Vice President, Physical Plant Safety

Now try rewriting the letter yourself in a friendly and informal tone. Change or remove pompous phrases while retaining as much of the meaning as possible. Our first draft follows. How does it compare with yours?

FIRST DRAFT

January 23, 2020

Richard McKinney
Fogg Warning Systems
773 South Rodeo Drive
Los Angeles, CA 90000

Subject: Approval needed for repair of smoke alarms

Dear Mr. McKinney:

Thank you for your prompt reply to my phone call describing our problems with our Fogg smoke alarms. As you are aware, it is necessary for the safety of our patients and our entire staff to have an extensive and dependable smoke-warning system. Because your customary repairman, Al Besto, is unavailable, we must hire a nonwarranteed service firm to maintain the system.

As you asked, I am sending a list of the rooms where the breakdowns occur most frequently. I am also enclosing a copy of the hospital floor plan on which I have noted the areas that have had different types of breakdowns. You'll notice that in some rooms (circled in red) the alarms ring at 20-minute intervals, obviously disturbing the quiet that patients need.

Also, another problem has come up since last week. On several smoke detectors, the flashing light that is supposed to come on with the alarm lights up independently from it. This has been particularly upsetting in Ward E, where many patients have complained about the flashing lights disturbing them late at night. We are sure that you find this situation as intolerable as we do.

Last, about the warranty: Clearly, we cannot wait for Al to repair the smoke-warning system, since he is extremely busy. Although I know that the Fogg policy normally covers expenses only when the repair work is done by our dealer, Al, I expect that the policy will be relaxed in this case, allowing us to hire another company. Will you please confirm this in writing?

Please call me about these pressing issues before Wednesday at 4:30 P.M. We appreciate your help.

Very truly yours,

Hiram Frost

Hiram Frost, Vice President
Physical Plant Safety

Rewriting the Fogg letter

It's important to write so that your reader understands exactly what you mean and knows exactly what action you expect. Use words that are precise and that imply action. In the Fogg letter, this straightforward approach worked as follows:

1. The subject line appears below the inside address to introduce the reader to the situation.
2. In the first paragraph we substituted plainer language to state the problem clearly.
3. In paragraphs two, three, and four we eliminated redundancies ("absolute"), pompous words ("said"), and overstatement ("countless"). We streamlined by weeding out useless words ("At this point in time") and overly dramatic phrasing ("hopelessly," "in this disturbing circumstance").
4. In paragraph four we clarified the action requested and changed the note of thanks from passive to active voice for greater impact.

Is there still room for improvement?

Yes. I think you'll agree that the following version of the Fogg letter is better than our first draft. Why? Because this version does more than just eliminate words or substitute one word or phrase for another. It uses a more natural, direct style, similar to what you would *say* to Richard McKinney if you were delivering the message in person. Also, we've added headlines and moved the bottom line to the top.

January 23, 2020

Richard McKinney
Fogg Warning Systems
773 South Rodeo Drive
Los Angeles, CA 90000

Subject: Please approve repairs to smoke alarms by Wednesday at 4:30

Dear Mr. McKinney:

Thank you for replying quickly to my phone call describing the problems with our Fogg smoke alarms. I appreciate your willingness to work with me to resolve these issues.

Actions requested by January 30 at 4:30 P.M.

1. Please call me to discuss the smoke-alarm problems before 4:30 P.M. on Wednesday.
2. If you can okay the exception to your policy, please initial this letter and return it to me by January 30 to confirm our agreement.

Exception to warranty needed because repairman is unavailable

Since our customary repairman, Al Besto, is unavailable, we must hire a nonwarranteed service firm to repair our system. We cannot wait for Al to repair the smoke-warning system. Although the Fogg policy normally covers expenses only when our dealer completes the work, I trust that Fogg will relax the policy in this case so that we can hire another company.

I've included the locations of the breakdowns

As you asked, I've attached a list of the rooms where the breakdowns occur most often. I've also enclosed a copy of the hospital floor plan and have noted the areas that have had different types of breakdowns. You'll see that in some rooms (circled in red) the alarms ring at 20-minute intervals, obviously disturbing our patients.

New Problem: Alarm lights are going on incorrectly

Another problem has come up since last week. On several smoke detectors, the flashing light, which is supposed to come on when the alarm sounds, lights up on its own. This has upset patients, especially in Ward E, where many have complained that the flashing disturbs them late at night. We are sure that you find this situation as intolerable as we do.

Thank you for helping ensure the safety of the patients and staff of our hospital.

Very truly yours,

Hiram Frost

Hiram Frost, Vice President
Physical Plant Safety

Adopt a contemporary tone

Fifty years ago, a formal tone was proper for business letters and memos. Today the polite formality of the past is often considered cold or snobbish. If, for example, you are writing to ask for someone's help, you don't want to sound distant. It's better to use the lighter and friendlier words of your daily speech.

The two e-mail messages on p. 109 were written by an office supervisor asking her employees for help in solving a problem. Which one do you think will receive a better response?

You probably agree that the second memo is far more likely to result in an amicable solution to the problem than the first. The second uses warmth and understanding to mobilize group spirit. The well-chosen tone shows that the writer understands how to motivate people. In the final sentences, she sets positive expectations, thus increasing the likelihood that her staff will cooperate.

From: Bea Bandera <bb@company.com>
To: Staff List
Subject: **Noise level in the break rooms**
Date: April 4, 2020

There has been great concern expressed about the growing tension between those personnel who use the break rooms as quiet places to work and those who go to the break rooms to converse. This conflict is counterproductive. The most pressing issue at hand is ascertaining the necessity of establishing quiet break rooms.

This developing tension between those who desire quiet and those who desire freedom to talk has great potential for unsettling the work environment and reducing productivity. It must be addressed without further delay. Suggestions deemed suitable should be submitted to the Human Resources Manager. This matter is of concern to all.

From: Bea Bandera <bb@company.com>
To: Staff List
Subject: **Noise level in the break rooms**
Date: April 4, 2020

How can we satisfy everyone?

Many of you have told me about the growing tension you feel around using the break rooms. Some of you go there to rest and socialize; others use the rooms to work quietly.

Your ideas are welcome

What do you think we can do to satisfy everyone? Should we designate one room as a lounge and the other as a quiet room?

We're sure you have other ideas

Since your feelings are important, please take a minute or two to send us your suggestions. If we work together, I'm sure we'll solve this problem.

Thanks for your cooperation.

Which letter will produce the desired result?

The following letters were written by two account executives from different advertising companies. Each was trying to convince Best Computers to contract with her company for an ad campaign. Read each one and decide which tone you feel is more persuasive. Then ask yourself the questions on page 111.

LETTER I

June 6, 2020

Mr. Sanford Blanchard
Product Development
Best Computers, Inc.
1234 Via Mallorca
San Diego, CA 94654

Dear Mr. Blanchard:

Having a great deal of experience working on advertisements suitable for the computer industry, my company, Van Snell Advertising Agency, wishes to inform you as to the optimum methods for the planning and execution of a successful advertising campaign.

In the past we have been able to assist other computer companies lacking the expertise or the facilities to create an advertising campaign to successfully reach their intended market. Most companies are, of course, aware of the successful campaigns we have developed in the past and of the prestige associated with the Van Snell Advertising Agency, but a brochure describing our team approach to advertising design will be found enclosed.

I trust that this proposal will be of interest to you, and that we can arrange a meeting with you soon.

We look forward to meeting you.

Very truly yours,

Ruth Van Snell

Ruth Van Snell
Account Executive

June 6, 2020

Mr. Sanford Blanchard
Product Development
Best Computers, Inc.
1234 Via Mallorca
San Diego, CA 94654

Subject: A plan to help you make the XL90 famous

Dear Mr. Blanchard:

Your new laptop model, the XL90, is an important addition to the family of high-quality Best computers already improving the lives of its users. But without a well-planned and carefully executed advertising campaign, the XL90 may fail to reach its entire potential market.

My company, Goodman Advertising Agency, is one of the oldest and most successful in the country. Our experienced and talented team of marketing research analysts, graphic artists, and writers are skilled in developing the finest campaign for each product they handle.

May I tell you more in person?
I would appreciate the opportunity to meet with you and discuss how our team may be of unique service to you. I will be in your area June 15 at 2 P.M. I'll call soon to see if you have time for a short meeting.

Cordially,

Alice Goodman

Alice Goodman
Account Executive

Marketing Letter Q&A

1. Which letter do you think was more influential?
2. List four words describing the first letter.
3. List four words describing the second letter.
4. On whom does the writer focus in the opening of Letter 1?
5. On whom does the writer focus in the opening of Letter 2?
6. Which approach is more likely to involve and engage the reader?
7. Which closing is more likely to result in a meeting? Why?

Compare our answers in Appendix A to yours. Pay special attention to the answer to Question 7. Try to adopt similar closing methods for your letters. They work!

Take the positive approach

Sometimes your tone carries a hidden message. Are you aware that between the lines you communicate your self-confidence or self-doubt to the reader? Ideas expressed positively are most likely to be positively received. To obtain the results you desire, you must convey an attitude of confident expectation.

Avoid *no* and *not*

Some people are always cheerful, self-assured, and optimistic. They express themselves positively, both orally and in writing. Many of us, however, tend to express ourselves more negatively—and most of the time we don't even notice how negative we sound. But if you tend to write "Do not waste energy" instead of "Conserve energy," then you are taking a negative approach.

"Don't take a negative approach!" is our message to you, but it would be better to say, "Be positive." It is always more persuasive to suggest what you want than what you don't want. For example, which closing do you prefer?

> Perhaps you won't object to my suggestions. Maybe you'll try to spot negative words and replace them with something less negative.
> or:
> I hope you'll agree with my suggestions and replace negative words with positive ones.

On your own: Look over some of your recent letters and e-mails to see if you suffer from the negative approach. An abundance of *no*'s and *not*'s is your signal. Watch for this weakness in future writing.

Use the "you" attitude

Involve your readers from the beginning by focusing on their needs, not your own. Discuss the product, service, or information you are offering from their point of view. Don't just list the benefits of your new product and leave your readers to decide what's in it for them. Instead, say, "*Your* problems will be solved by new product features." Tell them, "We will meet *your* needs, ensure *your* productivity, and make *you* a success in your organization."

Finally, avoid the angry e-mail or memo

Although it can feel cathartic to *write* when you're angry, it's never a good idea to *send* what you've written in the heat of the moment. If you need the release, go ahead and vent your anger on the screen—then save your document until you and the situation have cooled.

When you have calmed down, examine your audience and your purpose objectively. Which tone will accomplish your ultimate purpose:

- passionate?
- neutral?
- distant?
- conciliatory?

Edit your communication accordingly and send it with confidence.

Are you satisfied with your tone?

Are you satisfied that it is right for your audience and reflects a positive approach? If your answer is yes, take another step in the right direction by making sure you're writing at the right level for your reader.

Measure the readability of your writing

When you measure readability, you're determining how easy or difficult it is to understand your writing. By controlling the reading level, you minimize the risk of being misunderstood.

Software programs make measuring readability easy

Most word-processing programs come equipped with a grammar checker that can evaluate readability. Another option is stand-alone readability software. Programs such as Readability Calculations and Rightwriter check for features like number of syllables per word and words per sentence. They use different readability indexes to determine how easy your document is to read.

At what level should you write?

That's like asking how fast you should drive. The answer, of course, depends on the situation. However, the "when in doubt slow down" principle applies to writers and drivers alike. When in doubt, make your writing easier to read, not harder.

We recommend a readability level of 9 on Fry's Readability Graph for business writing. This standard avoids long words and keeps sentence length under 20 words. This book is written at level 9, and many of the sample documents we've used have a readability level of 7.

Adjust readability based on your reader and purpose

In business, it's powerful to know how to adjust for readability. You may find yourself writing everything from a summary report for a manager, to a feasibility study for engineers, to a set of procedures for data-input trainees. If you have several readers or you don't know who your readers are, stay around level 9. If you suspect that your audience may lack time, interest, or enthusiasm, make your writing as easy to read as possible, no matter how educated or senior they are.

Reading levels of familiar publications

The following list presents the readability level of familiar periodicals and documents:

The Atlantic	12 (difficult)
The Wall Street Journal	11
The New York Times	10
Time	10
The Boston Globe	10
This book	9 (strive for this)
USA Today	7
People	6 (easy)

How to measure readability

To derive a readability score on your own writing, refer to Fry's Readability Graph in Appendix B.

The problem of technical writing

Sometimes when you're writing on a technical subject, you cannot simplify the level of your writing even if you want to. If your readers are familiar with the subject matter, you probably shouldn't worry. But if you're trying to communicate technical information to nontechnical managers, stockholders, or clients, be extremely careful to define or translate terms they may not recognize.

You're not writing to entertain or to prove your literary talent

Business writing is not literature. Readers of business documents go to the subject line and the purpose statement, and they may or may not read more than the first sentence of every paragraph. They want to get the point quickly. You are writing to express, not to impress.

Are you satisfied with the readability of your writing?

If so, then there's just one step left to finalize your draft. This last step ensures the clarity and accuracy of the document you send to your readers.

6. Final proof

Proofread as if your career depended on it. It might! Sending out a letter without proofreading carefully beforehand is like walking into an important meeting elegantly dressed—except for those scuffed running shoes you wear on your morning walk to the office. At best, people will think you're not good with details. Is this an image that will advance your career?

For a high-stakes document, ask a colleague to use the *"Be Your Own Editor" Checklist* to proof your work for errors.

Read your draft slowly and carefully to spot errors

You must read at a pace that allows you to understand every word. If you read too quickly, you'll miss spelling errors like the simple transposition of letters in the following sentence:

> This technology is based on the latest in unclear research. (*Unclear* instead of *nuclear.* Note that spell check would not catch this error.)

Run the spell-check function religiously, but don't rely on it to catch all errors.

Look for errors in grammar and punctuation

You don't need to be an expert in grammar and punctuation to write. You already know more than you might think about correct English because you hear it every day in the news media. Try reading your draft aloud—you might hear many hard-to-catch mistakes.

Boost your grammar confidence level

Part 5 of this book is partially devoted to instruction and exercises in grammar and punctuation. Use the Grammar: Quiz Yourself section of part 5 (see p. 217) to review the basics. There are practical exercises, too, in case you have trouble with grammar or punctuation.

Remember your Step 6 checklist

You've come to the end of the editing process. Keep in mind, the *"Be Your Own Editor" Checklist* makes an excellent desktop reference for editing your documents. Use it to produce a final draft that presents your ideas in the best possible light. The more you use the checklist, the more automatic the editing process will become. Soon editing will be a comfortable habit rather than a tedious chore.

Who's responsible?

Passing the buck is often easier than accepting responsibility. The assistant will say that the writer ought to proofread; the writer will say it's the assistant's job. If your name is on the bottom of a letter, you are ultimately responsible for correcting every misspelling, typo, or grammar and punctuation error—in short, every detail.

Each piece of writing that leaves your office reflects your thinking, thoroughness, and success. You are sending an image of yourself into the world. You'll find that the more polished and neat your correspondence, the more respect you'll gain. Save yourself needless embarrassment: appear as successful as you are!

PART TWO

Writing Presentation Documents™

The great artist is the simplifier.

—HENRI-FRÉDÉRIC AMIEL

Writing Presentation Documents™

Asuccessful presentation captures your audience's interest and turns it into enthu-siasm for your proposal, product, or solution. To accomplish this goal, a presen-tation must focus on the needs of the *audience*—not primarily on your own.

If you have read Part 1 of this book, Reader-Centered Writing® is already a familiar con-cept to you. For presentations, however, we have adapted the six-step writing process for the specific needs of audiences, not readers. A listener, after all, is not a reader who can refer to earlier sections of a document—an audience at a presentation needs more repetition to retain your key message and bottom line. Organizing a presentation, there-fore, requires a different strategy from organizing a document.

How is a presentation different from your daily documents?

When we say a presentation requires a different strategy, we don't mean starting it by opening PowerPoint and creating slides, or simply cannibalizing past presentations for text and graphical content. PowerPoint abusers produce boring or incoherent presenta-tions because they don't stop to analyze their audience, define the purpose of the pre-sentation, or think creatively about their delivery documents.

Many salespeople, for example, are guilty of this lack of forethought. They open four old presentations and assemble a series of likely looking slides. Beyond attaching the same background to each slide, they pay little attention to text flow, stylistic continuity, or graphic unity. Even worse, they may produce a generic presentation that does not respond to the needs of their particular customer group or audience segment.

The result? An audience that is bored or confused, and therefore inattentive

Avoid these problems by following the Eight Steps to Audience-Centered Presentation Documents. Use the *Presenter's Blueprint* that follows to plan and outline the opening, body, and close of a presentation. This process will help you

- prepare presentation documents that reinforce your message
- generate and assemble content according to a simple, productive process
- sequence ideas strategically and persuasively
- decide which information to include on slides, transparencies, or handouts—and how to present it.

"Oh, no," you think, "not again. *Eight* steps this time? I just mastered six! And a *blueprint*? That sounds like a lot of work—I don't have the time for this." Rest assured that quite the opposite is true. This process is not only a proven time and energy saver, it is also designed to produce a coherent, audience-focused presentation. The continuity of text and unified graphic design will capture the attention of your audience and motivate them to accept your proposal, buy your product, or take the actions that your solution (recommendation) requires.

It's not a speech

Don't write—and then read—a speech as your presentation. Every bit of information you have to impart should not be projected onto the screen, no matter how elegantly you do it. The job of building a persuasive argument falls on you, not on your visual aids. And you will be persuasive only if you stop reading text and begin interacting with your audience. The very idea might fill you with dread. "That's no good," you think. "If it's not on the screen, I'll forget to say it." But if you have thoroughly rehearsed, your well-designed slides will not only hold the audience's attention—they will also act as helpful prompts for a persuasive presentation.

Nor is it a report

If you fill your pages with information that stands alone without your facilitation as a presenter, then you're writing a proposal or a report, not a presentation. If you do choose to write a stand-alone report in PowerPoint form, do it right. Design it to meet the needs of an audience of readers rather than listeners. For PowerPoint reports that are strictly on paper, see "Report Credibly" in Part 3.

The *Presenter's Blueprint*

The *Presenter's Blueprint* is a simple yet powerful tool that will help you outline and organize even the most complex presentations. Use this format, in combination with the eight-step process that follows, for every presentation you give, and you will create a compelling bottom line that your audience will remember after they leave the room.

The three-part structure of the *Presenter's Blueprint* is organized around the opening, body, and close of a presentation. Below, in the column on the left, we list the components that you should discuss in your presentation. On the right, we offer suggestions on how to display the component visually.

Opening: Preview Your Message

	Show
1. Grabber	Illustrate your grabber with an image or prop.
2. Bottom line	State your solution orally or graphically.
3. Purpose	State the specific goals for the presentation.
4. W.I.F.M. (What's in it for me?)	Capture your audience's interest with an image.
5. Credibility statement	A visual can be self-serving here—use with care.
6. Preview/agenda	Show an agenda slide.
7. Timing Include on the agenda slide.	
8. Transition	A transition slide is optional.

Body: Deliver Your Message

Use a modular arrangement to add content that explains or defends your message. Include as many modules as you need to present and support your argument.

Module #1	*Show*
1. Overview and impact of module	Illustrate the message of the module with an image.
2. Supporting data	Use charts, graphs, and tables as needed to present your data.
3. Wrap	A module summary slide is helpful.
4. Transition	A transition slide is optional.

Module #2: Repeat the preceding format.

Module #3: Repeat the preceding format.

Close: Review Your Message	
	Show
1. Overview and impact of module	Illustrate the message of the module with an image.
2. Bottom line	Repeat your "bottom line" slide from the introduction.
3. W.I.F.M. (What's in it for me?)	Repeat your W.I.F.M. slide from the introduction.
4. Call to action: next steps	This is your last slide; use a memorable image.

The Eight Steps to Audience-Centered Presentation Documents

The *Presenter's Blueprint* gives you a pattern for outlining and organizing content. How do you assemble this content into a persuasive presentation that will motivate your audience to act—to accept your proposal, carry out your solution, or purchase your product or service? Follow the Eight Steps to Audience-Centered Presentation Documents.

This process will help you produce the two types of presentation documents that are essential to any persuasive presentation. They include

1. Planning documents:
   - *Presenter's Blueprint*—the outline of your talk
   - *Presentations Focus Sheet*™—your audience-analysis tool
   - Start-up Strategy—the tool you use to generate content.
2. Delivery documents:
   - slides or overhead transparencies
   - handouts
   - speaker's notes.

Use planning documents during Steps 1–5, as you prepare your talk. In Steps 6 and 7, design and produce delivery documents—the visuals to show and handouts to distribute during the presentation. In Step 8, rehearse using the delivery documents you designed.

The Eight Steps to Audience-Centered Presentation Documents

PREPARE YOUR PLANNING DOCUMENTS

STEP 1: Set your goal and analyze your audience.
Use the *Presentations Focus Sheet™*.

STEP 2: Generate content for the presentation.
Use a Start-up Strategy such as
- a traditional tool like questioning or brainstorming
- a special presentation tool like a storyboard or notes pages.

STEP 3: Outline the opening.

STEP 4: Outline and sequence the body.

STEP 5: Outline the close.

PREPARE YOUR DELIVERY DOCUMENTS

STEP 6: Draft your delivery documents.
- Identify opportunities to use them.
- Decide on the best type.
- Draft each delivery document:
  —visuals
  —handouts
  —speaker's notes.

STEP 7: Edit your delivery documents.
Use the
- *"Be Your Own Editor" Checklist*
- Presentation Checklist.

PRACTICE YOUR PLATFORM SKILLS

STEP 8: Rehearse your presentation.
- Practice delivery.
- Practice using each visual aid.
- Determine when to distribute handouts.

Step 1: set your goal and analyze your audience

As in any writing task, your first step is to fill out a *Focus Sheet*. We have tailored the *Focus Sheet* from Part 1 of this book to the specific needs of presentation audiences. Analyzing your audience and defining your goal is vital to oral presentations—not just written documents. You can spend hours designing PowerPoint slides, only to find out that you bored your audience with a presentation that did not respond to their specific needs.

A tale of woe—and a happy ending

To convince you how important it is to analyze your audience, we'll tell you a story that we often hear.

Jim left the conference room knowing he had lost the sale. Hearing the executives say, "Thanks, we'll look it over and get back to you" had told him that much. As he walked across the parking lot to his car, he replayed his presentation on ChainPro's supply-chain software in his head.

He had told them about every feature there was to tell for the ChainPro system—how seamlessly it would integrate with their existing enterprise systems, how effectively it allowed various enterprises to collaborate, and how detailed its inventory tracking features were. He had hammered home how ChainPro was leaps and bounds above the competition—and it was! It would have vastly improved the supply chain of the prospect that had just turned him away. He knew it would have solved all of their problems.

Yes, it would have solved their problems, had he only focused on what they were. Jim realized his mistake as he drove back to his office. He knew his product inside and out—but did he understand his audience equally well? He hadn't taken the time to analyze his potential clients and figure out a bottom line and "so what?" that was specific for their needs. If he had, he would have been able to stress the benefits that had interested them in the first place.

Instead, he had overloaded them with endless details about features they weren't particularly interested in. The oversight was huge—and Jim could have kicked himself when he figured out how easy it was to fix.

At his next presentation to Zedcorp three days later, Jim walked into the Executive Briefing Center with a smile. He began by asking his clients, "What would you think about a proven system for lowering inventory on hand by 50 percent? ChainPro software can make it happen." By focusing on Zedcorp's pressing needs, Jim left the room two hours later knowing that ChainPro was at the top of the vendor list.

The *Presentations Focus Sheet*

The *Presentations Focus Sheet* is designed to prevent Jim's error. If he had used one the first time around, he might not have lost the sale. It's worth spending the minutes it takes to fill it out!

PRESENTATIONS FOCUS SHEET

1. Purpose/goal

   A. What is the goal of my presentation? _____

   _____

   B. What do I want my audience to think, believe, or do? _____

   _____

   C. Is my goal realistic given the time allotted? _____

   _____

2. Audience

   A. Who is the audience? _____

   B. What are their roles? Who are the decision makers? _____

   _____

   C. Why are they attending? What are their expectations? _____

   _____

   D. What do they already know about my topic? What *don't* they know about my topic?

   _____

   _____

   E. What's in it for them? Why should they listen? _____

   _____

   _____

   F. How will my topic affect them? How will the audience react? What objections will they have? _____

   _____

G. How will the audience use this information? _____

_____

H. What cultural issues could affect this presentation? Ethnic? Corporate? Language? Social?

_____

3. Bottom line

A. If the audience were to forget everything else, what one main message do I want them to

remember? _____

_____

B. *So what?* What is the impact of my bottom line? _____

4. Strategy

A. Should *I* be the presenter? At this time? _____

B. Would a phone call or one-on-one meeting be more effective? _____

C. Is the audience ready and able to act? If not, should I redefine or limit my goal? _____

_____

D. Do I need to make a series of presentations to achieve my overall goal? _____

_____

E. Is someone else communicating the same information? Should I check with that person?

How did that audience respond? _____

_____

F. If this is a team presentation, how can we best complement one another? _____

_____

5. Logistics

A. What are the times and location? _____

B. Who is my on-site contact? _____

C. What is the expected or desired presentation medium? _____

D. Is my technology compatible with on-site technology? _____

An audience is often a diverse group, with varying power levels, roles, skills, and knowledge about your topic. Some may be key decision makers; others are present just to gather background. Also consider different levels of receptivity: is *every* audience member ready to accept your solution or buy your service? Gather all the information you can about your audience before you begin to design your presentation, and be sure to answer the *Focus Sheet* questions for each type of audience member.

Here's an example

Jim filled out a *Focus Sheet* for his Zedcorp presentation as follows. It prevented him from repeating the mistakes that had lost him the previous sale.

Presentations Focus Sheet

1. **Purpose/goal**

   A. What is the goal of my presentation? *To impress upon Zedcorp prospects that our ChainPro software is what they want.*

   B. What do I want my audience to think, believe, or do? *Believe we can meet their needs; buy ChainPro.*

   C. Is my goal realistic given the time allotted? *They may not buy on first visit. Revise goal to: generate enough interest for another meeting; add us to their short list of vendors.*

2. **Audience**

   A. Who is the audience? *Executives flying in from Zedcorp.*

   B. What are their roles? Who are the decision makers? *Top VPs—Ramona Brown is the key figure, but she listens to her team members and stakeholders. Also attending is vice president James Wong from the L.A. office.*

   C. Why are they attending? What are their expectations? *To review our new ChainPro software release—they are not happy with their current system, especially with inventory exposure.*

   D. What do they already know about my topic? What *don't* they know about my topic? *They know we were rated #1 by ChainGain magazine and that we are well respected in the industry. They don't know exactly how our newest features will make a huge difference for them.*

E. What's in it for them? Why should they listen? *ChainPro is not the cheapest, but will give them greatest value and long-term return. It will make them more competitive and solve their most pressing problem: inventory exposure.*

F. How will my topic affect them? How will the audience react? What objections will they have? *They will be cool, impartial, reserved. They may have heard about a minor system instability that we have since fixed.*

G. How will the audience use this information? *To decide whether we are in the running for their vendor list.*

H. What cultural issues could affect this presentation? Ethnic? Corporate? Language? Social? *Zedcorp resulted from a merger of an Asian and U.S. company. New company has two very different cultures, views of needs, and approaches to solutions. I need to plan for that.*

3. **Bottom line**

A. If the audience were to forget everything else, what one main message do I want them to remember? *Purchasing ChainPro should be a strategic priority because it addresses one of Zedcorp's top three strategic goals. ChainPro will fix their biggest problem: inventory exposure.*

B. *So what?* What is the impact of my bottom line? *ChainPro will put Zedcorp ahead of almost all of their competitors.*

4. **Strategy**

A. Should *I* be the presenter? At this time? *Yes to both.*

B. Would a phone call or one-on-one meeting be more effective? *Not in this case.*

C. Is the audience ready and able to act? If not, should I redefine or limit my goal? *Done!*

D. Do I need to make a series of presentations to achieve my overall goal? *Probably. I'll add organizing a follow-up meeting to my goals.*

E. Is someone else communicating the same information? Should I check with that person? How did that audience respond? *Alice sent them information during the initial contact. I should call her to be sure I know about everything she sent them.*

F. If this is a team presentation, how can we best complement one another? *Maybe I should invite Carmela from the Chicago team. She had some particular implementation experience that matches Zedcorp's issues.*

5. **Logistics**

   A. What are the times and location? *February 2, 10 a.m., Executive Briefing Center.*

   B. Who is my on-site contact? *Jeff Bines.*

   C. What is the expected or desired presentation medium? *PowerPoint.*

   D. Is my technology compatible with on-site technology? *Not applicable—they're coming here.*

Step 2: Generate content

Choose a Start-up Strategy that works for you. You may already have a preferred one from the Six Steps to Reader-Centered Writing®—questioning, brainstorm outline, traditional outline. (See Part 1, Step 2, on p. 19.) Or try one of these strategies targeted specifically at presentations:

- storyboards—by hand or on the computer
- PowerPoint notes pages.

Storyboards

A storyboard is a visual outline of your presentation. You can create a storyboard either by hand or in PowerPoint. Handwriting is actually the better method as a Start-up Strategy since it allows you to write and sketch quickly without getting distracted by PowerPoint options. Starting with a pad of unlined paper (or a blank presentation screen), write down your main arguments. Put each one on a separate page: you will combine, subordinate, and sequence arguments later. Include simple graphics: just sketches, at this point, for charts or images that you will develop in Step 6.

A handwritten storyboard looks like this:

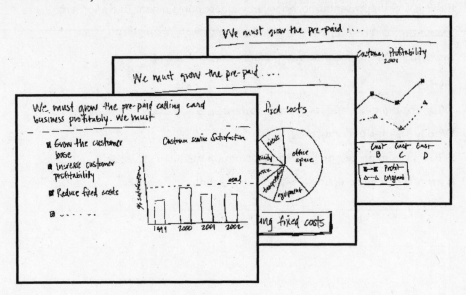

Remember that you are not designing slides yet but rather getting your big-picture thoughts down on paper or the screen. Don't worry about consistency in style and place-ment of graphic elements now; your purpose in Step 2 is to generate content, not to or-ganize and format it. That comes later, when you apply the *Presenter's Blueprint* in Steps 3–5. Design issues should not sidetrack you—concentrate on concepts rather than de-tailed content. The goal of Step 2 is not to get it right but to get it written.

PowerPoint notes pages

The notes-page view of PowerPoint is also a good way to generate content. Begin by giv-ing each of your arguments its own page. You don't have to start at the beginning. As in the free-writing Start-up Strategy, write down headlines, concepts, facts, anecdotes—anything that comes to mind regarding your topic—in any order. Use as many or as few words as you need to record your ideas. If you are able to at this stage in the process, label the page with the main argument and the section it represents: is it part of the grab-ber? Supporting data? Call to action?

In Step 4 you will sort, organize, and resequence your notes pages according to the *Pre-senter's Blueprint.* In Step 6 you will fully develop the content for each slide. Don't lose your train of thought at this point by getting bogged down in the details of fleshing out your slides.

Step 3: Outline the opening

Whatever effect you wish to have on your audience, it begins here. You want to take control of the room from the very beginning of your presentation, before you even project your first slide. Using the *Presenter's Blueprint,* create an opening that

- captures your audience's attention
- establishes credibility and rapport with the audience
- motivates the audience and generates interest in what is to come
- obtains audience buy-in for the length and purpose of the presentation
- orients your audience to the organization and format you will use.

The *Presenter's Blueprint* includes the following elements in the opening of a presentation:

1. Grabber

Open your presentation by grabbing your audience's attention. However you structure the grabber, make sure it is directly related to your topic. Here are some successful techniques for engaging your audience and motivating them to listen:

- *A rhetorical question:* "If I could guarantee you foolproof firewall protection, what would that mean for you?"
- *A real question:* "How many of you have guaranteed firewall protection today?"
- *A quote:* "As Winston Churchill said during the darkest days of World War II, 'Never, never, never quit.' "
- *An anecdote:* a real or imaginary story illustrating the value of what you're about to say.
- *A startling statistic:* "Ten million dollars are lost every year on . . ."
- *A demonstration:* to introduce a new policy, dramatically drop a copy of the old policy in a wastebasket.
- *Humor:* to lighten the mood and increase receptivity—but don't tell a joke unless you are convinced of your ability to make your audience laugh.

2. Bottom line

Deliver your solution (recommendation or conclusion) in one or two sentences. Also include the "so what?" from your *Focus Sheet* here. The "so what?" tells audience members why it's important for them to take action. For example:

> Our company's firewalls are inadequate. If we don't implement better security in the next quarter, we run the risk of compromising our proprietary data—and the competitive edge we've worked so hard to achieve.

3. Purpose

Don't keep your audience in suspense—tell them, right up front, what you hope to achieve with this presentation. Clearly stating your specific goals now will keep them focused and expectant.

> We will review our current firewall strengths and weaknesses to help you see why we need to upgrade *now*.

4. W.I.F.M. (What's in it for me?)

From the start of any presentation, the audience sits there thinking, "What is this speaker trying to accomplish?" and "What's in it for me?" Your most important task, in your opening, is to capture your listeners' interest. Do this by telling them what's in it for them. If you have a talk that you frequently repeat, such as a sales presentation, it is critical to tailor the W.I.F.M. to each specific group.

The W.I.F.M. isn't always obvious, as it is in "This software will be a real time-saver for you." For some members of the audience, what's in it for them is being the first to know about a new technology, so they can appear knowledgeable to their managers and peers. Or perhaps they will gain the knowledge to forecast a trend. Even for something as simple as budget approval, the W.I.F.M. might not be "You'll benefit from this new technology if you approve the budget for it." Rather, it might be "You'll look like heroes for your foresight in predicting this need and acting upon it."

5. Credibility statement

Why should your audience take you seriously? Mention your experience, research you've done, or special success related to your topic, but don't brag.

6. Preview/agenda

On a slide or flip chart, briefly outline the body of your presentation. Help the audience follow you by stating how many points you will cover.

7. Timing

Tell your audience how long the presentation will last and when breaks are scheduled. Include specific times on the agenda slide if possible. Audience members will then give you their full attention rather than wondering when they can return phone calls or check their e-mail. Also let them know if you welcome questions throughout your talk or only at the end.

8. Transition

Let the audience know that the preliminaries are over and signal that you are ready to begin the main part of the presentation.

Your blueprint notes might look like this

Remember Jim and his Zedcorp presentation? This is his *Presenter's Blueprint* for the opening of his talk.

Time Allotted	THE OPENING	Slide	Handout	Flip Chart
1 min.	**Grabber**	✔		
	What would you think about a proven system for lowering inventory on hand by 50 percent? ChainPro software can make it happen.			
3 min.	**Bottom line**	✔	✔	
	One of Zedcorp's top three supply-chain management (SCM) priorities is reducing inventory exposure. ChainPro gives you the solution to this challenge, and to many others that you face. We can measurably improve your management of supply contracts and build end-to-end supply-chain visibility. "So what?": ChainPro will put you ahead of almost all of your competitors.			
2 min.	**Purpose**	✔		
	To familiarize you with ChainPro and to demonstrate its potential benefits to Zedcorp. By reviewing your company's needs, I will explain why and how ChainPro will give you the competitive edge you seek.			
2 min.	**W.I.F.M.** (What's in it for me?)	✔		
	Of all SCM systems on the market, ChainPro is the easiest to implement. With our open, modular software architecture, we can have you up and running in half the time of standard SCM systems.			

Time Allotted	THE OPENING	Slide	Handout	Flip Chart
2 min.	**Credibility statement**	✔	✔	
	As you know, our company is one of the most highly respected in the industry. Along with being rated #1 by *ChainGain* magazine, we were also instrumental in the technological successes of three world-renowned Wealth 500 companies: Apex, Acme, and Summit. We have the expertise and experience to meet your needs better than any other company.			
4 min.	**Preview/agenda/timing**	✔		
	In the next hour and a half, I will show you how Zedcorp can profit from the ChainPro solution. Our SCM system will 1. reduce inventory exposure 2. measurably improve the management of supplier contracts and relationships [Break—15 mins.] 3. build end-to-end supply-chain visibility Wrap-up and final Q&A: 15 mins.			
2 min.	**Transition**	✔		
	Let's begin with Zedcorp's biggest inventory challenge: keeping inventory low while maintaining high levels of customer service—in short, inventory exposure.			

Step 4: Outline and sequence the body

Keep the promises you made in the opening. You must provide just enough of the right kind of information to flesh out your bottom line for each particular audience. A good body

- presents a strategic series of main points supporting your bottom line
- logically builds the proof your bottom line requires
- showcases the credibility of both you and your ideas.

The body of your presentation convinces your readers to accept your bottom line. You will succeed if you build a series of arguments and explain or support them with data. As you begin to outline the body, consider each point or argument you are making as a stand-alone section (or module), with a clear beginning, middle, and end. Include as many modules as you need to support your bottom line.

Use your *Focus Sheet* to sequence modules strategically—from most to least important based on your audience's needs. Each module should lead your audience toward acceptance of your bottom line. Limit your content; don't include more information than you need to prove your point just because you did the research.

As a bonus, a modularized presentation allows you to

- show how each module supports your bottom line
- reuse individual modules in other presentations
- make last-minute cuts and changes
- obtain understanding or agreement on the main point of the module before going on to the next
- quickly move on to another argument if you have everyone in agreement.

Module organization: follow the *Presenter's Blueprint*

Construct each module like a pyramid. Each primary argument—a solution or conclusion based on your analysis of the facts—presents the summarized message of the module at the tip of that module's pyramid. Below the tip, evidence in support of your argument is arranged from left to right, in descending order of persuasiveness.

The further down you move from the tip, the more supporting information you provide. Whereas you summarize your evidence for your bottom line near the top of the pyramid, your secondary arguments and supporting data should be closer to its base (see chart on p. 136).

1. Lead with your primary argument

Overview the argument by stating the message of the module and why it is significant to this particular audience, for example:

> The first way to reduce costs is to switch suppliers. My research will demonstrate that significant savings are possible as soon as you make this change.

2. Secondary arguments and/or supporting data

To support your primary argument, you must provide at least a secondary level that may consist of either arguments or data. Secondary arguments are solutions or conclusions based on fact analysis that persuade your audience to accept the key message of your module. Anticipate that your audience will ask "*Why?*" about each supporting argument. Respond to the *whys* until you can deliver factual data that you believe will address your audience's most important *whys*. Your facts should be collectively exhaustive—in other words, they should explain the problem or variation as completely as possible.

All arguments (secondary or even tertiary) must be defended by facts—supporting data. When you find yourself delivering data, you have fully defended your argument.

Your pyramid should look like this:

A Logically Persuasive Presentation

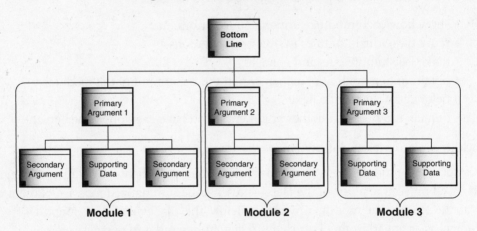

Sell your bottom line with well-supported arguments.

Other ways to sequence supporting data within a module

Although "bottom line on top" is the best choice for selling your ideas and making a memorable presentation, there can be occasional exceptions to this pyramidal module structure pictured above. Sometimes one module needs a different method of development. Here are four other ways to organize information besides the B.L.O.T. order. Choose the best method of development for each supporting argument according to the point you are trying to make.

Organizing Method	How It Works	Pros and Cons
1. Chronological order	• Makes your point by recounting a series of events • Requires a strategy (a color, graphic, gesture, or anecdote) to emphasize the key events	• *Pro:* works best with informative sections like background or implementation plans • *Con:* easily produces information overload, so apply the W.I.F.M. test
2. Bottom line on bottom	Builds up to your bottom line by presenting the support first	• *Pro:* effective for more resistant or skeptical audiences • *Pro:* useful when audience is less knowledgeable about your topic • *Con:* audience can easily miss your major message

3. Comparison and contrast: "whole-by-whole" order	1. Option A
	  • Advantages
	  • Disadvantages
	2. Option B
	  • Advantages
	  • Disadvantages
		• *Pro:* best for a more general discussion of each choice
		• *Pro:* best when kept to a single page in a report or a three-slide-maximum module

4. Comparison and contrast: "point-by-point" order	1. Advantages (first point of comparison)
	  • Option A
	  • Option B
	2. Disadvantages (second point of comparison)
	  • Option A
	  • Option B
		• *Pro:* best for an in-depth analysis of similarities and differences between two options

Using statistics, examples, and testimony to support your argument

Here are some tips for using three major forms of supporting data: statistics, examples, and testimony.

1. Statistics should be
   - honest: don't change the meaning by taking quotes out of context
   - representational: use a large-enough sample to be statistically significant
   - visual: "the size of a football field" is easier for the audience to grasp than "300 feet"
   - brief: share only those statistics that are new or critical to illustrating or proving your point
   - collectively exhaustive.

2. Examples can be
   - real: draw from your own or others' experience
   - hypothetical: give an example that could happen.

   Make sure your examples are accessible; offer words and concepts the audience can relate to in style and content.

3. Include testimony from
   - experts: make sure the authority is highly regarded
   - peers: in some cases you may have to request permission to quote.

3. Wrap

Summarize each module by restating your argument and the data you have presented to support it.

> As you can see, we can save $4 million a year by changing suppliers.

4. Transition

Before continuing, make sure your audience understands the key argument of the module. If appropriate, obtain agreement on an action. Then signal clearly that you are moving on to your next module and starting a different point.

> What do you think? Shall I go ahead? . . . Now, let's go on to look at a second cost-cutting idea.

Here is Jim's blueprint for the first module of his presentation.

Time Allotted	THE BODY: MODULE 1 REDUCE INVENTORY EXPOSURE	Slide	Handout	Flip Chart
2 min.	**Overview and impact**	✔	✔	

You asked if we can decrease Zedcorp's inventory exposure. Over the next five years, ChainPro can offer you impressive savings by
• reducing inventory on hand by 50 percent
• reducing out-of-stocks at the point of sale by 20 percent
• improving inventory accuracy by as much as 8 percent

20 min.	**Supporting data**	✔	✔	

1. **Reducing inventory on hand by 50 percent**
ChainPro achieves these results by
• optimizing inventory balance across warehouse locations
• automating the supplier reordering process with flexible business rules
• providing real-time visibility into the status of incoming orders.

2. **Reducing out-of-stocks at the point of sale by 20 percent**
By offering robust integration with downstream ordering and point-of-sale systems, ChainPro ensures you sell only what you're sure you can deliver.

3. **Improving inventory accuracy by 8 percent**
ChainPro will improve inventory accuracy by
• seamlessly integrating with all leading infrared inventory-tracking systems
• offering manifest functionality that ties to third-party shippers
• providing work-flow tools for managing inventory counts.

Software demo. Would you like a brief demo of our software solution?

Time Allotted	THE BODY MODULE 1 REDUCE INVENTORY EXPOSURE	Slide	Handout	Flip Chart
3 min.	**Wrap**	✔		
	As you can see, ChainPro will decrease Zedcorp's inventory exposure in three ways: • lowering inventory on hand by 50 percent • reducing out-of-stocks at the point of sale by 20 percent • improving inventory accuracy by as much as 8 percent. By using our next-generation supply-chain management system, you will achieve a projected savings of $15 million within the next three years.			
5 min.	**Transition**	✔		
	Do you have any questions? *(Limit Q&A to five minutes.)* Now that I've demonstrated how ChainPro will reduce your inventory exposure, let's move on to your next concern: measurably improving the management of supplier contracts and relationships.			

Step 5: Outline the close

This is the moment of power! A good close

- provides the real "take-away"—don't skip it, even if you're short on time
- persuades the audience to act
- nails down the next steps—the audience's roles and responsibilities.

A stirring finish is as important as a strong start. Use the close to reiterate your bottom line, imprint it on your audience's memory, and motivate them to move forward.

Again, follow the *Presenter's Blueprint* by including the following elements in the close:

1. Summary

Recap your arguments in support of your bottom line.

2. Conclusion

Your conclusion should include the following sections:

- brief review of the bottom line to confirm agreement, on one slide
- implementation plan, summarized on one slide (put the full plan in an appendix).

3. W.I.F.M.

Recap for your audience any individual or departmental benefits they might receive by accepting your bottom line. Pave the way for a compelling ending that your listeners will remember after they leave the room.

4. Call to action: next steps

Tell your audience the next step: what they should do *tomorrow*. If possible, obtain closure or agreement on some next steps to follow or implement.

Jim drafted his close as follows and achieved his goal: making it to the top of Zedcorp's vendor list.

Time Allotted	THE CLOSE	Slide	Handout	Flip Chart
5 min.	**Summary**	✔		
	One-minute summary of each module. Any final questions?			
5 min.	**Conclusion**	✔		
	• By incorporating our proven techniques for turbocharging your supply chain, ChainPro will dramatically decrease your inventory problems. Our SCM system will 1. reduce inventory exposure 2. measurably improve the management of supplier contracts and relationships 3. assess the effectiveness of your supply chain. • We'll increase your profitability by an estimated $15 million over the next three years.			

Time Allotted	THE CLOSE	Slide	Handout	Flip Chart
	• Preview of two-month implementation plan. (Pass out handout at end.)	✔	✔	
1 min.	**W.I.F.M.**	✔		
	Of all supply-chain management systems on the market today, ChainPro is the easiest to implement. We can have you up and running fast!			
2 min.	**Call to action**	✔		
	Install our software's free, 30-day trial demonstration and see the remarkable results for yourself.			

Step 6: Draft your delivery documents

You have planned, sequenced, and finalized your presentation outline or storyboard. Now it's time to draft your delivery documents—the visuals you will use during the presentation, the handouts you will distribute for later reference, and your speaker's notes.

Visuals

Visuals can include slides, overhead transparencies, and flip charts. If you are using slides and transparencies, you will, of course, produce them before the presentation. If you are using flip charts, you can design them beforehand or, if they are very brief, create them during the presentation.

What's the best way to make your point visually?

Each type of visual you choose offers three options for making a point:

1. Text
2. Pictures (clip art, illustrations, diagrams, or photographs)
3. Charts, graphs, or tables

The most interesting and eye-catching, and therefore successful, presentations use a mix of the three methods of expression. Variety will help you capture your audience's attention, maintain their interest, and persuade them to act. Review your presentation for opportunities to use graphics. Consider, first of all, which method of expression best conveys a message, but be sure to add variety. Use layout, color, images, and movement to vary pace and design. Even if a pie chart is the best option for six slides in a row, choose a different method of expression to avoid boring your audience and losing their interest.

Finally, consider what's doable for the skill level and budget you have available. If your staff doesn't have the expertise to produce original artwork, settle for clip art rather than amateurish illustrations.

Consult our companion volume, the *Instant-Answer Guide to Business Writing* by Deborah Dumaine, for advice on creating and using graphics, charts, and tables.

Slides: just one part of the show

Don't use PowerPoint as a weapon of mass distraction. Slides are not the whole presentation—they are simply tools to improve communication. You, as the presenter, still have to convince the audience to accept your bottom line. The purpose of slides is to highlight key messages, not to display every specific item of information.

Keep your slides simple, clear, and consistent. The audience has to absorb the information you present in the space of time it takes to show the slide. Consistency will speed understanding. Design each slide around its key message. Ask yourself, "What is the main point I want to convey in this slide?"

Background

The slide background you use should be appropriate to your audience. Does it project the right image: conservative, cutting-edge, inspiring? Keep your *Focus Sheet* in mind when designing a background, and tailor it to your bottom line. Before finalizing the design, try it out with text, charts, and illustrations to make sure they are readable.

Text

Follow these guidelines for clear and simple communication:

- Include one message per slide. Leave complex information for handouts.
- Put a unique title on each slide.
- Write in phrases instead of complete sentences. Capitalize just the first word of the phrase.
- Follow the "6 × 6" guideline: no more than six lines of text with six words per line; eight lines/eight words for technical presentations.
- Use one or two readable, complementary sans serif typefaces, and make them large enough to be seen from the back of the room. A good size for text is 24 points.

- Avoid cluttering the slide with numbers that are too small to read—provide only the figures you need to make your point.
- Present information in bulleted and numbered lists. Use parallel structure—and vary the structure from slide to slide. Use numbers when you need to refer to specific points.

The following text is not parallel. Different grammatical constructions have been used in both the introductory sentence and the list itself.

> This group will conduct planning, data gathering and initiate efforts in these areas:
> 1. implementation strategy
> 2. analysis of market
> 3. develop business case
> 4. measurement program.

Here is the same text corrected for parallelism.

> This group will plan, gather data, and initiate efforts in these areas:
> 1. implementation strategy
> 2. market analysis
> 3. business-case development
> 4. measurement program.

Graphics

Insert illustrations or charts whenever possible, but only when they further the meaning of your presentation. Again, keep it simple. Overdone graphic effects with animation and sound can be a distraction, not a communication aid. Your audience may become so engrossed in—or annoyed by—your graphics that they lose their focus on the bottom line.

Color

A color scheme will unify your presentation. Use five or six colors maximum. Select colors that are appropriate to your audience's organizational image as well as your own.

Here's an example

Compare message, background, text, and graphics in the before-and-after slide examples on pp. 145 and 146.

There are several messages in the "before" example: divide them into one message per slide. The uninformative title and body text are the same size, and the phrasing in the

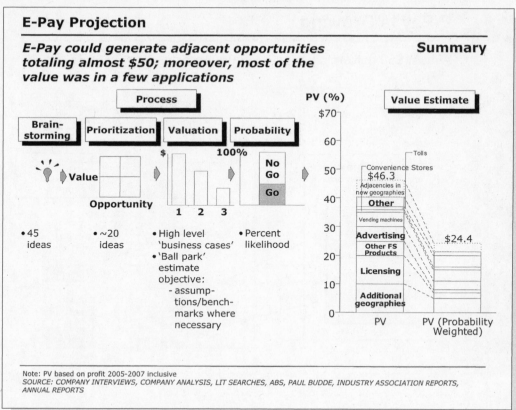

E-Pay Projection

E-Pay could generate adjacent opportunities totaling almost $50; moreover, most of the value was in a few applications

Summary

body text is too complex. Two complicated charts on one slide add to the graphical chaos. Finally and perhaps fortunately, since the slide is so busy, it lacks a background that would unify the presentation.

Now, look at the "after" slide. Its one clearly presented message, with main points highlighted, has impact. The informative title stands out. Body text has been shortened and simplified to state the message clearly. The single chart is easy to understand, especially with helpful captions. A simple background adds unity to the presentation and a professional touch overall.

Overhead transparencies

Transparencies have a flexibility that slides do not. They are easy to resequence or show more than once when your presentation is under way.

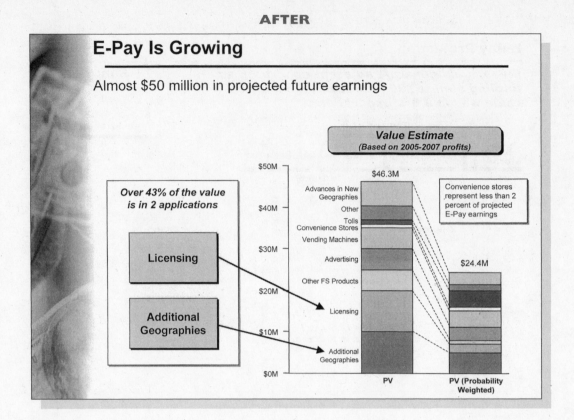

Most of the previous slide guidelines also apply to transparencies. Here are some additional tips:

- Put your transparencies in slip sheets. The clear sheet will help you center each transparency on the projector, and the white borders give a finished look on the screen. You can also write speaker's notes on the slip sheets.
- Number your transparencies in case you drop them.
- Instead of displaying a blank screen, shut off the projector when you're not discussing the transparency.

Flip charts

Flip charts are especially flexible. You can make them ahead of time or as you present, easily adding information and audience comments while you speak. They can also be combined in a presentation that uses slides or transparencies. Creating a visual as you speak is a great way to capture your audience's interest, but you must be exceptionally well rehearsed. Your words should flow effortlessly as you

- write quickly but legibly, in printing large and dark enough to read from the back of the room
- distribute text and drawings evenly, with an eye to white space
- use colors to emphasize different points, and alternate colors for easier reading.

Above all, maintain eye contact with your audience—never talk to the flip chart. If your charts are complicated, prepare them ahead of time so you can focus on the audience.

Handouts

Print and projection are two very different media. Be wary of using slides as handouts—and vice versa. Your slide may be too abbreviated to be useful as a handout, while your handout will often contain too much information to be a successful visual.

Once you have defined your purpose and planned your visuals, consider the type of handouts you will need. Limit their number—a thick sheaf of unnumbered pages probably won't get read at all. Distribute handouts only when you're ready to discuss them. To avoid a roomful of heads-down readers who are focusing on paper instead of on you and the screen, give a big-picture overview *before* distribution.

If you are distributing slide printouts, make sure that each slide is clear and easy to read when transferred from a large and animated color screen to a small, static, black-and-white sheet of paper. Consider your audience carefully. When discussing a high-level marketing concept or selling a clear and simple strategy, don't distract your audience with paper. For complex or technical data, you will probably want to distribute slide printouts at the start of the presentation so that listeners can add their own notes.

Speaker's notes

Even the most experienced presenters may need a memory aid when presenting complex or unfamiliar material. Remember that you aren't writing a speech; you don't need complete sentences of polished prose in well-constructed paragraphs. *Brief* speaker's notes, either typed out in PowerPoint notes pages or jotted down on index cards, will

- help you remember facts, figures, and complex data points
- prompt you to make smooth transitions between slides
- remind you to repeat or review information in a long and complex presentation.

Reading speaker's notes, however, is as bad as reading from the screen. Keeping them brief will prevent you from focusing on paper in your hands rather than on your audience. The key to a smooth presentation is not extensive speaker's notes but complete preparation and practice.

Step 7: Edit your delivery documents

You have finished the free-flowing, drafting step in designing your presentation. Now it's time for the critique that will correct and refine your presentation documents. As with any writing project, get some distance before you begin editing. Take a break. If possible, postpone editing for 24 hours.

Editing guidelines

Follow these general guidelines for editing titles, body text, graphics, and charts:

1. **Titles** should be meaningful, not a statement of the obvious. Focus audience attention by emphasizing the bottom line. Write a single phrase that does not exceed two-and-a-half lines.
2. **Body text** should provide analytical or factual support for the slide title. Write short and simple sentences or phrases that are parallel, and use the active voice. Limit yourself to 3 bullet levels and 36 words per slide.
3. **Graphics** should make a point, not provide decoration. Make sure they are appropriate to the subject and the audience. Maintain consistency in style; don't mix clip-art cartoons with photographs.
4. **Charts** should explain statistical relationships more clearly than do words. Their purpose is to save your audience time by delivering the message without extraneous facts. Use charts to capture the attention of audience members—they are more likely to study and remember a well-done chart than a paragraph, no matter how elegantly written.

The greatest challenge of using charts is choosing the one that will best convey your message. Use the Graphing Advice Matrix on p. 149 to help you decide which chart is best suited to your needs.

The *Presentation Checklist*

When you return to your presentation, review it thoroughly. Is it audience-centered? Have you incorporated all the elements of the *Presenter's Blueprint*? Have you built in enough transitions and repetition to keep your audience on track? Apply the *"Be Your Own Editor" Checklist* (p. 69). Then use the *Presentation Checklist* on p. 150 to ensure that your talk will be both lively and memorable.

Step 8: Rehearse your presentation

You've worked hard and designed a top-notch presentation—but it can fail if you skip Step 8. No matter how good a presenter you are, you have no way of knowing if your

Graphing Advice Matrix

If your message is about…	Your 1st choice might be…	Your 2nd choice might be…	
Parts of a whole	Pie Chart	Column Chart	
Time series or trends	Line Chart (Many data points)	Column Chart (Few data points)	Area Chart (Few data points)
Comparisons across categories with no natural order	Bar Chart	Column Chart	Line Chart
Comparisons between two or more variables	Column Chart (Few data points)	Line Chart (Many data points)	HLCO Chart
A cause-and-effect relationship	Scatter Chart	Scatter Chart with Trend Line	
Hybrid or combination (overlays)	Line & Column Chart	Area & Column Chart	
Numerous data points	Formatted Table	Multiple Columns	
Quality Measurements	Pareto Chart	Process Control Chart	
Interrelationships of a process	Flow Chart	PERT Chart	Gantt Chart
Dispersion of a data set	Column Chart	Box Chart	

Presentation Checklist

Strategy of presentation
- ❏ Visuals in best places in the presentation?
- ❏ Visuals customized for audience?
- ❏ Most effective medium: slide, transparency, flip chart, handout?
- ❏ Variety of expression: text, picture, chart?

Sequence of presentation
- ❏ Agenda up front?
- ❏ Organization follows the agenda?
- ❏ Best method of organization for each module?
- ❏ Transitions included in speaker's notes?

Content of visuals
- ❏ Stresses meaning, not just data?
- ❏ Exactly complements what you plan to say?
- ❏ Clearly makes one main point?

Design of visuals
- ❏ Follows 6 × 6 rule (6 lines down and 6 words across)?
- ❏ K.I.S.S. ("Keep it short and simple") applied?
- ❏ Print large and legible enough?
- ❏ Fonts limited to two?
- ❏ Background matches purpose and content?
- ❏ Consistent in layout, color palette, and graphic style?
- ❏ Chart types appropriate to data?
- ❏ Chart elements clearly labeled: table rows and columns, chart axes?

talk is within the time limit without a rehearsal. Practice assures a smooth delivery and improves your powers of persuasion.

Are your slides in the right sequence? Do they give you enough prompting? Have you built enough transitions and repetition of key points into the presentation? All these questions will be answered in a practice session. Your confidence will increase because you know when to use each visual and when to distribute each handout without interrupting the flow of the presentation.

A well-rehearsed presenter focuses on the audience, not on reading notes or the screen and fumbling with handouts. Even the most seasoned presenters practice to make sure that an insecure delivery will not sabotage the hours spent creating a persuasive and sophisticated presentation.

PART THREE

Challenges of Persuasion

The difficulty is not to affect your reader, but to affect him precisely as you wish.

—ROBERT LOUIS STEVENSON

Report Credibly

There are many different kinds of reports. Are you documenting the outcome of a project, summing up your sales team's achievements, providing a comprehensive study of all work done in a certain area, or recommending solutions to a problem? Your style, tone, and approach will vary according to the purpose of your report.

Are you writing a presentation or a report?

Slides are the medium of choice for a presentation, but they don't convey a message well on paper. An audience that is reading doesn't have the benefit of interaction with a presenter who can expand upon and discuss the information on the page. The solution is not simply adding extra detail to your presentation slides and printing them. Don't leave the task of assembling and synthesizing your content and all-important bottom line to your readers—that's not the way to persuade them.

Reports in PowerPoint

Use PowerPoint if your company or client requires it, but keep in mind that you're writing an on-paper report, not a presentation. Organize your report according to the guidelines in this chapter rather than using the *Presenter's Blueprint* (Part 2). Above all, don't omit the all-important executive summary from a long report. Listing a few bullet points as a preview, as you might do in a presentation, is not enough to orient busy readers to your content.

Since you are preparing a document that will be read, write in complete sentences instead of the brief phrases suitable for a presentation format. Many pages of light text on dark are difficult to read, so use black text on a light background instead. Rather than the large font size that is readable when projected on a screen, use 11- or 12-point text. And choose a serif rather than a sans serif font—it's easier to read on the printed page.

What type of report are you writing?

Use your *Focus Sheet*™ to analyze your readers and define your purpose. Find out how much detail your readers expect and how technical your language can be. Your reason for writing a report will help you decide which report format to use: formal, informal, or letter. A discussion of all three follows, but first let's look at some common types of reports. Consult the *Instant-Answer Guide to Business Writing* by Deborah Dumaine for a complete description of each type.

- A *problem-solving report* provides solutions (or recommendations) to business challenges.
- A *strategic report* offers a blueprint for growth to a company or division.
- A *feasibility report* presents a concept and analyzes its economic or technical feasibility.
- An *investigative report* analyzes a topic and discusses the results of your research. It presents comparative facts, conclusions, and, if appropriate, solutions.
- A *progress report* describes the status of a project in progress.
- A *completion report,* on the other hand, presents a comprehensive record of a completed project.

The main parts of a formal report

A formal report, which usually requires extensive research and planning, is intended for a wide readership. Distinct guidelines govern its structure, although companies do vary in their standards. Some are rigid, while others allow the writer considerably more flexibility. In addition to the main sections, there are always subsidiary parts of a report, some of which are optional. The following sections are standard.

1. Transmittal letter or e-mail

A transmittal letter states the purpose of the report and previews findings. It is not usually detached from the report.

2. Cover

The report cover states the title, your company name and contact information, the client (if applicable), and the date.

3. Title page

The title page lists the title, author, company, date, and the client's name (if applicable). Often the cover doubles as the title page.

4. Table of contents

The table of contents shows readers how the report is organized. Include a list of illustrations, figures, tables, and appendixes with their page numbers.

5. Preface and acknowledgments

In this brief, optional section, thank those who contributed to the project.

6. Executive summary

The executive summary is a succinct presentation of your purpose, solutions, and supporting points. Use it in a report that is five pages or longer to convey your most important points to senior executives who may have little time to read any further. Once they have read the executive summary, your readers can skim the entire report, grasp the main point quickly, and concentrate on only those facts that are important to them.

Write the executive summary last. Include all your key points in the order you present them in the report itself. The executive summary should not, however, be a replica of your report in miniature. It does not need to contain all the same sections and should not exceed 10 percent of a long report's length.

Sometimes you need to write more than one executive summary: for example, one for management and one for technical experts. You may not be able to follow the sequence of the report exactly because you want to position your bottom line for maximum impact on the chosen audience. Be sure to indicate clearly where in the body of the report the content occurs.

7. Introduction and purpose of report

The introduction describes the purpose and scope of the report. Set the context, describe the reasons for the report, and preview your bottom line. Don't include too much background at the beginning—your more knowledgeable readers will lose interest. They are busy people; if you don't persuade them up front, they may not give you a second chance. Many managers tell us that they often read only the first few pages of a report.

8. Bottom line or solutions

Since the function of your report is to present solutions (or recommendations), hiding them at the end would be counterproductive. Start with your bottom line and proceed logically to the facts and analyses that support it. State the actions and procedures that you recommend.

Use the active voice and the first-person point of view. "We" is usually preferable to "I" because it indicates that the report represents the views of a team or the entire company.

9. Supporting argument and analysis

The sections you include in the body of a report depend on its subject. Typical sections include

- facts in support of your solutions or conclusions
- analysis
- discussion
- procedure or methodology
- implementation plan
- background.

Facts in support of your solutions or conclusions: Use a pyramidal structure called a logic tree to organize this section. State your solutions or conclusions at the top of the pyramid. Then organize your fact-based secondary arguments and supporting data on the levels beneath. Sequence them in descending order of persuasiveness from left to right. Your primary arguments (in summary form) are near the tip of the pyramid, secondary arguments closer to its base.

Make sure each supporting argument relates to the preceding solution. Almost all supporting evidence will answer the question "Why?" Anticipate other questions your readers may ask, and answer them as well. Continue through as many levels of argument as you need until your supporting arguments and data are collectively exhaustive—that is, they answer as close to 100 percent of your readers' questions as possible. (See the Logic Tree on p. 157.)

For more guidance on defending your argument in a complex, research-based report, click on *Bottom Line Thinking* at *writetothetop.com*.

Procedure or methodology: Describe your research methods in full technical detail. Use charts and tables to convey complex information quickly and clearly. If your *Focus Sheet* audience analysis showed that your readers may not be highly interested in this topic, put it in an appendix.

Logic Tree

Build a logic tree to support your argument.

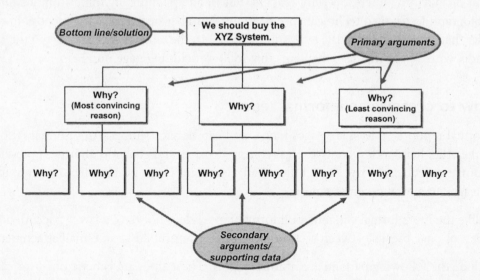

Background: Are you surprised that "Background" appears so late in the report? Writers often include background material simply because they've done the research—and because many writers open their reports with it. Wherever you present your background information, ask yourself if it's really vital to readers' understanding. If you're just recapping a bit of history your readers already know, move it toward the end of the report, include it in an appendix, or consider eliminating it altogether.

10. Conclusion and final summary

Your conclusion is not the place for new information: the main points of this section should follow logically from the body of the report. Take advantage of this final opportunity to convince your readers by restating your conclusions and solutions persuasively. Don't end with an uninspiring summary.

11. Bibliography or reference list

A bibliography is arranged alphabetically by the author's last name; a reference list is numbered sequentially to correspond with a superscript number in the text. Include a bibliography or reference list if you quote or paraphrase books, journal articles, Web pages, in-house reports, and any other written material.

12. Distribution list

This list of report recipients may appear in an appendix.

13. Appendixes

Appendixes include material that may not be crucial to the understanding of the document or may only interest certain readers. Put in an appendix anything from a simple photograph to detailed technical specifications. Number or letter each appendix in the order that you refer to it in the text, and include it in the table of contents. Begin the appendix with a page that lists the items that follow, including page numbers.

How to organize an informal report

A formal report is at least six pages long—and can be six volumes. An informal report, on the other hand, is less complex, less comprehensive, and generally shorter. It presents information concisely, with very little detail. Examples range from a memorandum to a colleague to a brief progress report.

Unlike the more formal version, an informal report does not have a cover page, divider pages, or page breaks between sections. It is often transmitted as an e-mail attachment.

Include the following parts in an informal report. These titles are generic only: for each one, write a more specific headline that expresses the message of the section.

1. **Title:** the results of your report stated in 6 to 12 words
2. **Introduction:** your purpose in writing and brief background information vital to the reader's understanding of the report
3. **Solutions or conclusions:** your key message or bottom line
4. **Supporting facts:** a discussion of your analysis and results defending your solutions
5. **Summary:** a recap of results and conclusions
6. **Next steps:** actions for the readers and other stakeholders to take

If you have successfully applied our advice on formal reports, then writing an informal one should present few problems. Your major challenge will be to sum up a considerable amount of information briefly but without sacrificing clarity of expression. The hardest aspect of writing an informal report is, in fact, keeping it short. As many a writer has said, "My report would have been shorter, but I didn't have the time."

What about letter reports?

A letter report is written on letterhead, with date, inside address, salutation, subject line, complimentary closing, and signature. The letter format is used less frequently now that many reports are sent electronically with an e-mail cover note.

It is usually better to separate even the shortest report from the cover letter. Reports have a wide distribution, including readers you may not have anticipated. The individual, relationship-building, and even personal parts of your letter would not be suitable for this segment of your audience. Save such comments for a separate cover letter to the audience you know well.

If you do decide to write a letter report, organize it as you would an informal report.

Reap the benefits of teamwork

A long and complex report is usually a team effort. To ensure smooth team functioning, consult the guidelines in Part 4. If several writers have contributed, an editor must review the final draft for consistency in style and visual design. Appoint a fact checker to verify accuracy, especially of legal or technical material.

Finally, ask someone who is not a member of the team to read the report before you submit it. A colleague who has not been obsessing over the material, as have you and your team, may offer valuable observations on report structure and the clarity of your presentation.

Write to Win Sales®

Your goal when writing to a customer or a prospect is to move the sale ahead by writing a Reader-Centered® document. Whether you're writing to start a relationship, get a meeting, raise interest, confirm needs and understandings, or close a sale, customer-focused writing keeps your name in front of your prospect. Use the Better Communications® approach to reduce your writing time—and gain more time for selling. After you have closed the sale, use the same techniques to maintain and deepen the customer relationship.

As for any document, follow the Six Steps to Reader-Centered Writing®. Begin by analyzing your audience and defining your purpose for writing. Understanding your audience—especially an audience of multiple readers—is especially critical to winning sales.

The *Sales Focus Sheet*™

If you're writing a fairly simple document like a follow-up letter, use the basic *Focus Sheet* on p. 12. A high-stakes proposal, however, requires more in-depth questioning that considers such issues as features, benefits, and impact of your product or service. To analyze these issues, use the *Sales Focus Sheet* that follows. If you have more than one reader (as a sales proposal usually does), answer the questions for each reader.

Sales Focus Sheet

1. Purpose

A. Why am I writing this?_____

B. What do I want each reader to do? (Action, attitude?)_____

_____

2. Audience

A. Who exactly are my readers? Group? Status?_____

B. What is each reader's primary role: Decision maker? Influencer? Implementer? Other?

_____

C. What are the readers'/customers' situation and needs?_____

D. What are each reader's primary concerns? (Business impact, financial, functional/technical, performance, service, support?) _____

E. What does each reader know about the subject?_____

F. How will each reader react? _____

G. What's in it for each reader? Why should the reader read this or agree with it? (Personal or business benefit?)_____

H. Which competitor is the reader considering?_____

I. What solution am I recommending?_____

J. Which features, benefits, and impact do I need to address? (See *FBI Worksheet* in this section.)_____

_____

K. What added value do I need to stress?_____

L. What obstacles or objects do I need to overcome?_____

M. How will each reader use this document?_____

N. What cultural issues could affect this communication? Ethnic? Corporate? Language? Social?_____

_____

3. Bottom Line

If the readers were to forget everything else, what one main message must the reader remember? (Impact of choosing/not choosing our company.) _____

_____

4. Strategy

A. What is the decision-making process? _____

B. Should I be writing this? At this time? Would a phone call or meeting be more effective?

_____

C. Am I too early? Or too late to send it at all? _____

D. Is someone else communicating the same information? Should I check? _____

E. Have I trimmed the distribution list to the essential readers? _____

F. Which method(s) of transmission should I use?

- ❏ Fax?
- ❏ E-mail?
- ❏ Internal mail?
- ❏ Videoconference?
- ❏ A meeting?
- ❏ A presentation?
- ❏ Internet?
- ❏ Postal delivery?
- ❏ Courier?
- ❏ Intranet (Web sites or shared folders)?
- ❏ Other? _____

What is a successful sales document?

To serve as a successful sales tool, your document should have

- impact
- customer focus
- strategic organization
- a reader-centered format
- a friendly and professional tone
- polite assertiveness.

How do you achieve these winning qualities? Let's look at each one in more depth.

Write with impact

Highlight only those product or service strengths that relate to your customers' needs. Show them the beneficial effects, implications, or consequences your product or service will have on their business—or to them personally. Go beyond features and benefits to *impact*. Make sure to answer the following questions:

- Why is this feature and benefit so important to *them*?
- What specific problem has the potential buyer expressed that the feature will solve?

Use the following *FBI Worksheet* to ensure the impact on a specific customer of key features that you are highlighting.

The *FBI Worksheet*

One of the biggest mistakes of salespeople, especially in the technical field: creating a *feature-oriented* proposal that discusses every feature in exhaustive detail. Instead, your proposal should be *reader centered*. You must listen to the customer's needs and stress the features that meet those requirements in terms of benefits to the customer.

A second mistake that many salespeople make: they stress the benefits of a feature to a prospect but leave out its impact, the "So what?" that makes the feature important to that particular customer—and clinches the sale. For example, the primary *feature* of the network service you're trying to sell to an international consulting firm is that it's wireless. The *benefit* is that the customer can access the network from virtually anywhere, without worrying about the accessibility or adaptability of electrical outlets and telephone lines.

What is the *impact* on the customer, whose consulting staff spends most of its time in countries with iffy phone service and intermittent power? Easy access to network services will speed communication, so customer responsiveness and productivity will rise. The *FBI Worksheet* helps you assess the benefits and impact of each feature on your specific audience.

FBI Worksheet

Features	Benefits	Impact
Characteristics, facts, data, information about product or service	How product, service, or feature can be used or can help a customer	Effects, consequences, and implications of benefits to *this* customer—the "So what?"

Much as you love every single feature of the product or service you are selling, keep your discussion customer focused. Avoid features and benefits that stress your own goals—focus on the prospect's instead.

Customer focus

When writing to customers or sales prospects, always take the "you" attitude. Show them that you are putting their concerns ahead of your own by presenting your product or service from their point of view. Use *you, your,* and the prospect company's name more than *I/we, my/our,* or your company's name. This technique is especially effective in headlines. Instead of "*Our* product provides faster service," write, "*You* want a product that meets *your* need for faster service."

Use the Questioning Start-up Strategy on p. 22 to put yourself in your customer's shoes. List, then answer, questions your prospect will have about your product or service. This strategy will also help you anticipate questions, respond to objections, and consider alternative solutions.

Strategic organization

Put the bottom line on top. Capture your readers' attention right away by showing that you have the best solution to their problem or need. Sequence content so that the prospect will agree to each key element as you present it. Include fees toward the end.

Reader-centered format

Use a format that encourages your prospect to read. Headlines and sidelines make your key points stand out and guide the eye down the page. Short paragraphs also add to readability, as do bulleted or numbered lists. Use emphasis—boldface, a contrasting font, boxes or shading—to highlight deadlines, action items, and cost savings.

Product descriptions, statistics, facts, features, choice of options, pricing variables: what sales document doesn't include all these items? They are difficult and boring to read in dense paragraphs of text. Use diagrams, illustrations, photographs, graphs, and charts to make this information easily digestible and even interesting to read. A certain amount of sophistication in page layout and graphic design can only impress your prospect with your professionalism and expertise.

You may think that cramming as much information as you can onto a single page reduces length and therefore makes your document easier to read, but that is not the case. Give your readers' eyes a rest, especially in long and complex proposals. Frame your ideas with white space: wide margins, plenty of space between paragraphs, between sections, and between headlines and text. Your customer will be all the more impressed by being able to read several pages quickly rather than one page slowly and laboriously.

See the discussion on visual design of documents on p. 73.

Friendly and professional tone

Be personable, as though you are talking to your prospect. Follow these guidelines:

- Avoid overly formal language and jargon. Use simple words. Explain acronyms and technical words the customer might not understand.
- Streamline your sentences and remove gobbledygook.
- Use the active voice and positive language—and remember the "you" attitude.

See the discussion on word choice and tone on p. 99.

Polite assertiveness

Don't be afraid to ask for the sale or to make it clear that you will be requesting the order. There's nothing wrong with being assertive, as long as you are polite. After all, your prospect is quite aware that you want to make the sale, not just provide information.

Make it clear what differentiates you from the competition. Don't leave your readers to make time-consuming comparisons on their own. Do it for them—without bragging or disparaging your competitors, of course.

The letter of agreement

Congratulations! You've reached an oral understanding with your customer, and now it's time to confirm your agreement in writing. Having negotiated successfully this far, you may feel that the final coup would be to maneuver the buyer into writing the contract or letter of agreement. Resist this temptation.

By writing the letter yourself, you retain more power over the situation. The subtleties of the agreement will be construed in your favor, and any issues that remain in doubt will be drafted from your point of view.

On the other hand, if you leave the agreement writing to the buyer, you are much more likely to end up in a weak position. You might have to renegotiate points that the buyer misunderstood or completely omitted, intentionally or not. You'll be much happier with the results of any negotiation if you reserve the writing of the agreement letter for yourself.

Let writing be your competitive strategy, not your competitive liability

Writing to make a sale is always irritating to the true sales professional, who loves to be out in the fray with the customer. The advice in this section and the ones it references will make your writing an asset that differentiates you from the crowd and gives you back precious time. It's worth the investment to try it!

Write a Persuasive Proposal

A winning proposal will convince your prospects that you understand their needs as well as or better than they do—and that your solution offers the best return on their investment. To persuade a potential buyer to choose you over the competition, you must do far more than simply provide a laundry list of information about the products or services your company offers.

Answer the customer's questions

Your proposal must answer the questions your prospects are asking, whether they have verbalized these questions or not:

1. Does your company understand our problem? Do you know our needs, issue by issue? How well do you understand our business and technology? Do you have a clear vision of the result we want?

2. How will your company solve our problem? How will your plan or product work? How long will it take? How much will it cost? What are your solution's benefits and return on investment?

3. How will you fill our need better than anyone else? What experience have your people had on similar projects? Do you have the expertise, management, facilities, and equipment necessary to achieve the desired result? How do you differentiate yourselves from your competition?

Formal or letter proposal?

Which should you write? Your decision will be based primarily on the cost and complexity of the project. Write a formal proposal when your plan is complex and the solutions costly.

Write a letter proposal if you have already addressed many of your prospect's questions or are fairly certain you are the only, or top, contender for the contract. A letter proposal may imply that you have virtually closed the sale and are writing mainly to confirm oral agreements. A letter proposal is also suitable when your solutions aren't overly complicated, so you can include all the relevant information within the scope of a five-page-maximum letter.

The main parts of a formal proposal

If you're responding to an RFP, your proposal may need to follow the customer's guidelines for topics, content, and layout. But in general, formal proposals include these standard sections:

1. Title page
2. Table of contents
3. Executive summary
4. Introduction
5. Proposed procedures (or technical plan)
6. Implementation plan
7. Qualifications
8. Cost analysis (or your investment)
9. Statement of agreement
10. Appendix

Consult Deborah Dumaine's *Instant-Answer Guide to Business Writing* for an in-depth discussion of each part of a formal proposal. The rest of this section will concentrate on a tool that is invaluable to any salesperson: the letter proposal.

A better letter proposal

A letter proposal is informal. If the deal is virtually closed, the letter documents oral agreements for your customer to review.

Parts of a letter proposal

The sections that follow are generic. Don't confuse them with the persuasive headlines you will need to include throughout your proposal.

1. Subject line. Use this chance to sell; include impact or benefits for the buyer in the subject line.

2. Friendly thanks. Begin by thanking your customers for inviting your proposal. Make a point of saying that your solution is based on your company and theirs working together.

3. Our understanding of your needs. Present a clear analysis: restate and define problems, and acknowledge the buyer's decision criteria. Tailor your headlines to show that you understand your customer's needs:

> **You are facing these challenges**
>
> **You seek to . . .**
>
> **You need . . .**
>
> **You asked about . . .**

Be sure to use the "you" attitude. Mention the customer more than you mention yourself, especially in headlines. *I* and *our* are not incorrect, but they indicate that you're more interested in selling your product than in meeting your buyer's needs.

4. Solution preview: Briefly summarize how you plan to meet your prospect's needs.

5. Benefits of solution: Highlight each need, then follow with the features and benefits that will meet that need. Don't just provide a list of every single feature—each one must match a specific customer requirement. Showing that you listened to the buyers' precise needs will help you sell your product or service.

6. Impact of solution: In this section, discuss the effects, consequences, and implications of each feature on *this* customer. Give your prospect the "So what?" that will clinch the sale.

7. *Solution in more depth:* You just previewed impact and benefits. Now discuss each feature or process in detail: let the customer see exactly what you will be doing, how you will do it, and why your method is best.

8. *Implementation plan:* Demonstrate that you have the necessary ability and resources to implement your solution. Include an action plan that allocates responsibility: what you will do; what the customer will do. Describe the major tasks or phases involved in implementation, and include a schedule of deliverables.

9. *Your investment:* List your costs and justify them. If you relate costs to deliverables, the customer will understand the breakdown and be more receptive to your overall figure. This is also a good place to explain the unique qualifications of your company to deliver on the proposal. Add a paragraph on key players or company experience.

10. *Attachment preview:* Include a bulleted list of attachment contents.

11. *Suggested next steps:* Create a sense of urgency to entice your readers to act quickly. Include an assurance that you'll call soon to go over the proposal with them, answer questions, and talk about the next steps.

12. *Thank you:* Express your eagerness to work together with a warm, personal tone. A headline is optional for this section.

13. *Attachments:* Attachments can include

- an implementation schedule
- background data related to solutions and conclusions
- company brochures and biographies
- copies of your contract or purchase agreement.

A sample letter proposal from Better Communications follows.

Subject: Danskill-Crosby Group's winning leadership-development program will contribute to Zedcorp's continued sales success

Thank you for meeting with us on May 15 to discuss Zedcorp's sales-leadership development needs and our solutions. We are excited by this opportunity to work with you to develop your global team and achieve sales growth.

Our understanding of your needs

You are struggling to expand the success of your global sales-leadership team while winning new business in an increasingly competitive market. You know that developing this team's effectiveness is vital to

- deepening relationships with current clients and growing your business with them
- seizing new sales opportunities—by outselling your competitors
- keeping and attracting good people
- negotiating profitably
- finding new strategies in a volatile economic climate.

You understand that developing your leadership team's ability to provide vision and practical strategies for client management and sales growth is a must-do initiative. You must improve two key areas to meet your clients' and prospects' needs better than your competition can:

- the leadership skills of your sales-engineering consultants
- the flexibility of the sales-management systems that support their work.

SOLUTION PREVIEW: Danskill-Crosby will harness its global industry experience and proven methodologies to help you reach your goals

We propose to partner with you to ensure that your sales-leadership team, consultants, and sales-management systems fully support your company's client focus and goals for growth and profitability. To ensure that you get the best possible results from your people and systems, we will put our firm's broad industry knowledge and in-depth experience to work for you.

Our solution has two parts.
1. Leadership solution:
   - a competency assessment
   - a behavior profile for leadership success
   - an assessment and coaching program
2. Systems solution:
   - strategies for continuous improvement
   - our *DC LeaderSell System*

The benefits of strengthening sales leadership at Zedcorp

You understand that meeting the developmental needs of your sales leaders and supporting them with leading-edge sales systems will help your company

- keep and expand your leading industry position
- grow your customer base by communicating the value of your service solutions
- strengthen Zedcorp's ability to respond nimbly to new opportunities and challenges
- make your sales organization more productive in less time
- recruit and retain the best people for your sales team.

BUSINESS IMPACT: Your sales organization will increase revenue and profitability while continuing its leadership in the marketplace

To grow profitably, all businesses must do more with fewer resources. The Danskill-Crosby Group responds to that need. Not only do we help sales leaders support their people—we also achieve quantifiable growth in global sales as measured by our *DC LeaderSell System*. Our clients report these results:

- Over 76 percent of our sales leadership teams **increase face-to-face client time by 30 to 50 percent.**
- The *LeaderSell System* reduces information loss while **increasing cross-functional knowledge-sharing capability by 40 to 50 percent**—ensuring greater success in closing sales and effectively implementing client solutions.
- Team-sales engineering consultants estimate a **97 percent improvement in their ability to understand expectations and meet goals**—increasing their own job success and satisfaction.
- **Sales rise by up to 65 percent in one year**—because sales teams do a better job of communicating value and meeting client needs.
- **Client satisfaction more than doubles,** as measured by our innovative assessment tools.
- R.O.I.: Leadership coaching and systems improvements are **returning five to ten times our clients' investment.**

SOLUTION IN MORE DEPTH: How do we work?

Danskill-Crosby Group will establish consistent, useable, result-oriented sales-leadership systems and sales methodologies based on

1. Competency assessment. Through a series of in-depth interviews, we will identify the core competencies that your global sales-leadership team needs to succeed today—and develop for tomorrow.
2. Behavior profile for leadership success. Once we systematically identify core competencies, we will produce a behavior profile of outstanding sales leadership at Zedcorp.
3. An ongoing assessment and coaching program—for the length of our agreement with you. The program will be built around the core competencies essential for your sales-leadership team to succeed.
4. Recommended, useable strategies for continuous improvement, based on the behavior profile and the assembly of best practices emerging from the coaching program.
5. The proven *DC LeaderSell System,* which will help your sales team manage key information and provide up-to-date, easily accessible metrics on your sales-leadership practices and sales results.

HOW WE WORK WITH YOU: Our senior partners are at your service

We begin by assigning a team headed by one of our senior partners who understands your industry. Then we conduct in-depth interviews with your key leaders to understand not only their competencies but also your work, processes, successful strategies, and obstacles.

To ensure that you meet your leadership-development and sales goals, we tailor and implement a leadership-development plan that includes individual coaching, workshops, and ongoing leadership forums. Throughout, we work with you to review process, implementation, and results.

Your investment
During our meeting you preferred our FastTrack Intensive Plan with an ongoing two-year package of consulting, coaching, and assessment. We propose working with and coaching your Sales Leadership Top 25 and their sales-engineering consultants. The program includes systems assessment and implementations using our assessment tools.

Phase	To include	Your investment	Investment per sales unit
		$	$
		$	$
		$	$

WHAT'S ATTACHED?
You'll find:
1. *DC LeaderSell System* description
2. Client list
3. *Facts about Danskill-Crosby Group*
4. Ten-Year Cumulative Results Report: all clients
5. Proposed implementation schedule
6. Partner biographies
7. Contract copies (2)

Suggested next steps
I will call to discuss how you would like to proceed. We're excited about partnering with you to reach your goals for defining and delivering best-in-class service and products in your industry.

Thank you for considering us.

Make your prospects your collaborators

Potential buyers have a problem or need; you must convince them that you have the best solution. The more they see you as able to fix their problem, the more appealing you will be in their eyes. As you prepare your proposal, do your best to meet or at least speak with your prospects about their major needs. By asking for suggestions and inviting discussion, you'll learn more about their problems, fine-tune your solutions—and make collaborators out of them even before they sign the contract.

PART FOUR

Action Through Words

*The single biggest problem with communication is
the illusion that it has taken place.*

—GEORGE BERNARD SHAW

Energize Your E-Mail

Most of the world by now, it seems, relies on e-mail as a primary means of communication. Because e-mail is so easy and convenient, people tend to draft a message and press "Send" with little planning and no editing. That kind of message—with action items, next steps, and deadlines buried and unclear—only annoys and alienates busy corporate audiences. They'll read it only because they have to. To write a message that readers *want* to read, follow a simple three-step process.

Three steps to energizing your e-mail

E-mail is a powerful communication tool if you use it well. An audience-centered message that attracts readers will also get results. Our plan, draft, and edit process will help you write e-mail that drives action in record time.

1. Plan your e-mail

Filling out a *Focus Sheet*™ is necessary for long, complex, or information-packed e-mail messages. If that's the kind of e-mail you're planning to write, you should probably reevaluate your strategy. It might be better to attach a file to a short e-mail cover note. Few people have the time or the patience to scroll through several screens of poorly formatted e-mail text.

One subject per message, please

Don't send an e-mail message that covers more than a single topic. You may think you're doing your readers a favor by reducing the volume of incoming messages in their in-box, but you're not. A multitopic message, especially with an uninformative subject line like "Important issues to consider," is hard to read, harder to remember, and hardest to file. Don't expect your readers to respond to all your issues—most likely they will concentrate on just the first one or two.

Start with questions

Begin writing e-mail by asking yourself a few questions. You can record your answers right on the screen; they will serve as a Start-up Strategy and become the outline of your message. Many of these questions will be familiar from the *Focus Sheet* (see p. 12).

1. If my readers were to forget everything else, what is the main message I want them to remember? This is your bottom line. If you walked into your readers' office and stated your main message, what questions would they ask you? For now, list their questions on the screen. You will answer them later, when you draft your message.
2. Who, exactly, are my readers? Include not only the addressees but also other people likely to see your message. But don't fill in the address field yet. Addressing your e-mail should be the last thing you do, just before you send it. That way, you won't send a half-baked draft.
3. What is my readers' primary attitude: receptive, indifferent, or resistant?
4. Action requested: what do I want my readers to do?
5. What are the next steps?
6. What are the deadlines?

Develop headlines from your questions

Yes, e-mails need headlines! Don't omit this essential communication tool because "it's just an e-mail." Your on-screen readers deserve the same consideration and easy access to information as your on-paper audience.

Use all capital letters for headlines unless you're positive that your recipient's system can handle boldface type. As for any document, make your headlines as specific as you can, not generic.

Generic	*Specific*
Problem	**Problem: system down today**
Priority	**Today's staff meeting: top priority**

Recommendation	**Recommendation: accept the GigaTrix proposal**
Conclusion	**Conclusion: R&D project is not feasible**

Sequence your message

If your reader is receptive or indifferent to your primary message, put it first. If you fear the recipient may have a negative reaction, make a bad-news sandwich: put your bottom line between two slices of good news. (For more on sequencing for resistant readers, see the Step 4 discussion on p. 43.)

2. Draft your e-mail

Answer the questions you wrote down during your Start-up Strategy. Add other sections as needed, and label each with a headline. Headlines that drive action include

Deadline

Action requested

Suggested next steps

Who's responsible?

Thank you

The all-important subject line

Do your messages get lost in the volumes of e-mail your readers scroll through every day? Make sure yours are opened by including a subject line that is specific and informative. It should

- state the bottom line
- include an action step or deadline if possible.

Based on the subject line, which one of the following messages would you read first?

Billing: Hot May issues	**Meeting**
Billing issues	**4/12 meeting @ 2:00**
Pls pay attention to these billing issues	**Special guest at 4/12 meeting, 2 p.m.**

3. Edit your e-mail

You are almost ready to press "Send"—but take a minute to be sure that you don't embarrass yourself. Check content, sequence, design, structure, and tone. And proofread! Just run down this checklist quickly:

Content	Does the message cover a single topic?
	Will the subject line compel the recipient to read?
	Are action requests, next steps, and deadlines clear to the reader?
Sequence	Is the bottom line on top for receptive readers, strategically placed for others?
Design	Did you use headlines?
	Do action items and deadlines stand out?
Structure	Are paragraphs 6 lines maximum?
	Are sentences limited to 20 words?
Style and tone	Are words short and simple? Is your prose free of jargon?
	Have you limited your use of abbreviations, acronyms, and emoticons (smiley faces)?
	Is your style appropriate for the audience, informal yet professional?
	Did you use the active voice, a positive approach, and the "you" attitude?*
Final proof	Did you proofread?
	Did you spell-check?

An additional resource

Consult our companion volume, the *Instant-Answer Guide to Business Writing* by Deborah Dumaine, for tips on

- maximizing your subject line
- adding emphasis
- using abbreviations, acronyms, and emoticons
- observing e-mail etiquette
- avoiding e-mail abuse.

When *not* to use e-mail

Never send a message when you're angry. Think about the situation first, and then respond. Ask yourself, "Would I say this to the person's face?" "Can I be sure I won't regret

---

*See pp. 91, 111, 112 for more on these topics.

this when I see it in my out-box?" If the answer to one or both questions is no, then don't send it. Remember, each message is a record of your words—none of us wants to make permanent something we wish we hadn't written.

You should also refrain from sending an e-mail when you need to give corrective feedback, either personal or performance-related. Though praise translates easily to e-mail ("Chris, these graphics look great!"), corrective feedback does not ("Pat, you could have done better on this"). Such comments can easily be misinterpreted. Because the writer's intended tone is so difficult to determine in e-mail, criticism almost always sounds worse from the computer screen than face-to-face. If you have something corrective to say, do so in person.

Finally, consider stopping the e-mail meandering and using the phone. Though you and your long-distance colleagues have been sending a chain of e-mails back and forth, you have not yet found the solution to that nagging problem. Pick up the phone and hammer out a decision through spoken, not electronic, dialogue.

A novel idea: write a letter instead

And what about the good old-fashioned paper letter: is it going out of business style? Not at all! In fact, e-mail has become such an irritant that a letter often seems like a novelty. So, if you've tried again and again to get in touch with your prospect but have gotten nowhere electronically, consider a letter. A visually pleasing piece of paper could set you apart from your competitors and their relentless e-mail stream.

Write for the Web

When you surf the Web, do you read every word on every Web page that you visit? Of course not. In fact, people who visit Web sites are not even called readers; they're users. That's because most visitors to Web sites don't read. Instead, they scan. It's easy to see, then, why the challenges facing Web writers are different from those facing document writers.

In this section we'll answer these key questions about writing for your Web audience:

- *How do you design for an audience you can't control?*
  Web users don't follow a page from top to bottom. They click freely, rarely reading information in the order it's presented. In order to maximize the amount of pertinent information your users find—and keep them interested in your site—you need a strategic visual design.
- *How can your site answer questions fast?*
  Most of your users are just like you. They're short on time and in need of information quickly. They come to your site because they believe that there is something for them there—either to click on, scan, or learn—and they want to access that something *right now*. Catering to your users' needs will go a long way in ensuring satisfied visitors.
- *How will your Web site overcome user cynicism?*
  The Web is crowded with pages of ill repute, and users know they are connecting to unknown servers at faraway locations. Therefore, it is vital that you earn

their trust. Learn to use straightforward language, and your site won't be regarded as just another pop-up ad.

- *How can your Web site engage users to actually read your content?*
  As any scroll bar user will attest, it is much more difficult to read text on screen than on paper. In fact, when Web users do read, they do it about 25 percent more slowly on screen. That's why they scan—to get all desired information from merely a sentence or two, or even just parts of sentences. Limiting your content is the key.

Getting started

Envision your Web site with the objective, critical eyes of your potential visitors. What would they like to see? Knowing your audience and purpose will help you start designing an action-driving, *reader-centered* site.

To start planning your site and learning about your audience, take a *Focus Sheet* approach by answering these questions:

1. *What is the purpose* of your site? Sales? Marketing? Information? Education? Entertainment?
2. *What bottom-line actions* do you want your visitor to take? Contact you? Join? Buy? Believe? Complete and return your form? What's in it for them?
3. *Who is your expected audience* (your intended visitors)?
   - Are they young? Old? Male? Female? From your country?
   - Are they likely to be Web veterans? Novices?
   - Why is it in their best interests to buy, join, complete, etc.?

The more extensive your site, the more an in-depth reader analysis will pay off. Even a corporate departmental site may require some focus groups or surveys to be sure you really know your users' needs.

Keeping your users' needs before you, turn your focus to the four key elements of your Web site:

1. Content
2. Visual design
3. Tone and style
4. Ease of use

Since the Web provides more give-and-take than do other forms of written communication, you want your visitors to feel that your site offers a relationship of equals. Using these four elements in combination will help you create a truly navigable and inviting site that drives action.

Content is first

What's in?

Of course, your bottom line or key message is in. And it arrives first. On every page, state your message or conclusions early and directly, then create links to supporting information.

Interview your customers to gain insight into writing your Web content. Ask them:

- What are your needs?
- What information do you hope to gain from our site?
- What decisions are you making when you go to a site like ours?
- What is the first question you had about our company?

The answers to these questions will guide the content and structure of your site.

Since users scan rather than read, they look for links as visual signposts and trust them to provide credibility. Link users to a "deeper dive" into your content by including

- your rationale for your conclusions
- an analysis of your summary
- related sites that justify your claims
- background, history, and statistics.

What's out?

How much information goes into each section? Use a Start-up Strategy from Step 2 of the Six Steps to Reader-Centered Writing®—a brainstorm outline or questioning. Then, with your users' needs in mind, include only pertinent information that leads directly to the actions you want.

People must trust what you say, so leave out excessive promises and exaggerated claims. Users will be more impressed with credible testimonials from third parties or customers as well as case studies or statistics that demonstrate how you get results.

Visual design can make or break a site

Follow these guidelines for laying out your Web site.

1. Place your content in topical chunks—100 words or less in 2 or 3 paragraphs for each separate topic. This technique reduces the need for scrolling, which will undoubtedly win the gratitude of your visitors.
2. To repeat, Web users don't like to scroll. So keep each page short. If the purpose of your site is marketing or entertainment rather than education

or information, users will have even less tolerance for long sentences and paragraphs.

3. Help your users find answers more quickly by linking related pages that have a similar focus or objective. Do your best to imagine how your users' minds will work by clicking through a transaction you might expect from your most-sought-after user.

4. Attract your users with clear and dynamic headlines that shout "Read me!" Headlines will help users decide whether they need to read each section in more or less depth.

5. Use lists; they increase the visual appeal of your site because users prefer them to paragraphs. If your lists are too long for your Web page, provide links to them.

6. Include photos, diagrams, and charts—they all help your users understand more quickly.

7. Capitalize on your freedom to use font and color on the Web; it's an easy way to emphasize key words and links. But don't overdo it—two fonts and four colors are plenty.

Use a friendly tone and style

Tone and style are just as important on the Web as they are on the printed page. A warm and friendly tone and approachable, easy-to-read style will keep your users interested. As you edit your Web text, you should:

- Use simple, informal words.
- Limit the use of slang, metaphors, and idioms (especially if you have a global audience).
- Remember the "you" attitude: speak directly to your audience using the words *you* and *your*. It's all about your readers.
- Use the active voice—since the Web is an immediate connection to your visitor, the active voice generates interest. Feel free to use your company name and the corporate *we*.
- Edit, edit, and then edit again. Two lines is your maximum for complete sentences. A good rule: use half the number of words you normally would for hard copy.

Make it easy to use

A typical user enters a topic in a search engine and receives thousands of hits. Improve your Web site's chances of being viewed by making sure each page title or main heading relates to your target readers' needs or interests. Every page in your site needs a different title—40 characters is best but no more than 60. Generic terms are out, as are tired articles (*the*) and "Welcome to" titles—they hinder scanning.

Every page should have its own brief summary after the title. Use descriptive key words that express your page's main topic. Keep key words consistent: *income* on one page shouldn't be *revenues* on a second and *proceeds* on a third. Take advantage of the fact that many search engines show summaries below each page title. But be careful—search engines often truncate titles. Make your summary informative, but limit it to 150 characters.

When looking through search-engine results, every user has the same question: what does this page have to do with what I'm looking for? Your goal should be to answer this question at the top of all your pages. Make every page stand alone, and help your users find out immediately how it relates to their search.

Put your company name and contact information at the end of every key section. Don't lose a customer over that omission.

Finally, always make it easy to get back to your home page. Put a "back" button at the end of every section.

The Six Steps help users, too

Even though we've established that Web users are not readers, the Six Steps to Reader-Centered Writing still apply. Like any other document for people you wish to inspire to bottom-line action, a Web site requires planning, drafting, and editing. Apply what you learned in Part 1 to your Web pages, and you'll be on your way to a highly navigable site that drives action. Remember: the term *user-friendly* has never gone out of style.

Write as a Team

Major assignments such as research or audit reports, proposals, or position papers usually involve groups of people—not just individuals. Even if one person has primary responsibility for a document, several layers of review can precede approval and sign-off. You are writing on a team anytime more than one person must be involved before the document is final.

Some people find it difficult to write as a team. Others, especially experienced writers, welcome the opportunity because they recognize the value of others' input. Writing as a team allows you to capitalize on all the brains and talent available. By developing your team-writing skills, you will find both the process and the final product more satisfying.

What role do you play on the team?

From project to project, your assignment may differ. Even within one project, you might sometimes write, sometimes edit. Understanding the differences among roles will help all members of the team function at their best. These are the team-writing roles:

- The *delegator* is responsible for assigning tasks and approving the final product.
- *Writers* draft content.
- *Editors* may perform both a conceptual edit for content and a copy edit for grammar, unity of writing style, and consistency of document design. A single editor should be responsible for the final proof.

Clarify, communicate, coordinate, and critique supportively

Clarify roles

As basic as it sounds, sometimes teams don't have a clear understanding of who will be drafting, who will be editing, and who will be signing off on what sections. As soon as possible, assemble all involved members in a room, real or virtual, to clarify roles, responsibilities, and deadlines.

Communicate with the team

Delegators, writers, and editors need to communicate their expectations and concerns to one another. If you are having trouble with either your team members or your assignment, talk it out with those involved. Keeping your issues to yourself is almost always counterproductive.

Coordinate work

For efficiency, writers and editors need to coordinate their work.

Delegator:	Consult the writers before setting deadlines.
Writers:	Avoid making promises you can't keep. If you think a deadline is unrealistic, try to negotiate a new one.
Editors:	Be specific about the time you need to review carefully. Keep writers and delegators informed about your progress.

Critique supportively

It's important to comment honestly on one another's work. It's equally important to do so in a way that acknowledges people's contributions and builds confidence rather than destroying it. Later we'll offer specific tips on critiquing supportively.

Use the Six Steps as your common language

Keeping the preceding overview of the team process in mind, let's look at how the Six Steps will guide you through the group-writing effort. Experience proves that if the team completes the planning phases together, the writing and editing go far more smoothly.

Step 1: Completing the *Focus Sheet*

What is the most common complaint we hear from team writers? People waste countless hours on misdirected work because initial goals were not adequately explained. To prevent this, have your whole team (or at least the key players) meet to fill out the *Focus Sheet* that follows. This is an essential step at your first meeting for teams of *any* size.

Team Writing Focus Sheet

Answer these questions as the first step in any writing task.

1. Purpose

   A. Why are we writing this? _____

   B. What do we want the reader to do? _____

2. Audience

   A. Who *exactly* is our reader? Do we have more than one? _____

   B. What is the reader's role: Decision maker? Influencer? Implementer? Other? _____

      _____

   C. What does the reader know about the subject? _____

   D. How will the reader react to our main message: Receptive? Indifferent? Resistant? _____

      _____

   E. What's in it for the reader? Why should the reader read this or agree with it? _____

      _____

   F. How will the reader use this document? _____

   G. What cultural issues could affect this communication? Ethnic? Corporate? Language? Social? _____

   H. Should anyone else receive this? _____

3. Bottom Line

   A. If the reader were to forget everything else, what one main message do we want the reader to remember? _____

   B. *So what?* What is the impact of our bottom line? _____

4. Strategy

   A. Should our message be a document? Or would a phone call be more effective? _____

      _____

   B. Timing: Are we too early? Or too late to send it at all? _____

   C. Distribution list: trimmed to the minimum? _____

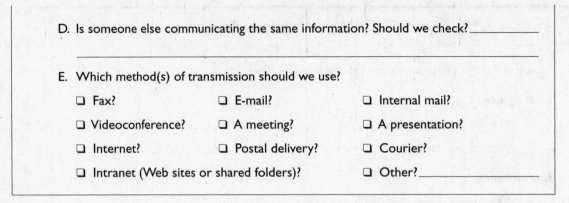

D. Is someone else communicating the same information? Should we check? _____

_____

E. Which method(s) of transmission should we use?

   ❏ Fax?   ❏ E-mail?   ❏ Internal mail?

   ❏ Videoconference?   ❏ A meeting?   ❏ A presentation?

   ❏ Internet?   ❏ Postal delivery?   ❏ Courier?

   ❏ Intranet (Web sites or shared folders)?   ❏ Other? _____

The vital questions on the *Focus Sheet* are *"Why are we writing this?"* and *"Who will be reading it?"* But it's best to answer all questions completely before you move forward. The more time you invest in Step 1—analyzing your audience and defining your purpose—the more time your team will save later.

What if you can't meet, even virtually, to fill out the *Focus Sheet?*

Delegator: Answer the key questions to get the team started with a clear understanding of the project. The *Focus Sheet* will help you minimize afterthoughts. Your writers inevitably have different writing styles, so give them a sample of the approximate tone and style you're after. Guide the team toward choosing what the audience needs and away from debates about whose style is best. Remind them that "ego is out, strategy is in."

Writers: If you have not been given clear direction, use the *Focus Sheet* to interview the delegator before you tackle the project. Ask any questions you have about roles, deadlines, or expectations. Then schedule a conversation for those among you who can get together. Each absentee can fill out the *Focus Sheet* individually and send it to the meeting.

Step 2: Generating ideas as a team

Delegator: Your participation is especially important in this phase; you may discover some content or ideas that haven't come out yet. The more you can be involved up front, the better.

Writers: Involve as many team members as possible in generating ideas. Use one or more of the Start-up Strategies. If the whole group can't get together, have each person work alone on a strategy. Then the team can compare notes and integrate a vision for the document.

Steps 3 and 4: Grouping and sequencing information

At this phase you create the outline that will guide the writing of the document. Until people have agreed on the skeleton, you are not ready to flesh it out. To complete this part of the process efficiently, limit to one or two the number of people who work on Steps 3 and 4. They can propose to the team appropriate categories and headlines for the content generated during Step 2. Then the team can work together to sequence and finalize an outline and submit it to the delegator for approval.

Efficiency tip: Save time with an Idea Draft

Both our audit and our business-development clients work on tight deadlines. To avoid wasting time perfecting a first draft without the manager's input, they use the Idea Draft. This outline or list of ideas presents the relevant content in a strategic sequence, showing the delegator the key concepts of the work in progress. The purpose of the Idea Draft is to get approval of the overall outline or plan for a document.

Typically, writers submit first drafts to be sure they're on the right track. If they learn they've omitted important facts or included irrelevant content, they're usually frustrated over all the time and effort they've wasted. The Idea Draft offers an advance check-in to prevent frustration.

When you use the Idea Draft, both parties make a deal. Here's how it works:

Delegator: Promises to comment only on the *content* and *sequence* of the Idea Draft; grammar and style come later. This form of supportive critiquing frees the writers to keep their part of the deal.

Writers: Agree to present the relevant points in a logical sequence, preferably in outline form.

The Idea Draft is particularly helpful when

- you need to speed up the process on routine writing assignments
- you have a complex or high-stakes writing project, such as a proposal
- you're just learning the job.

Step 5: Drafting as a team

Writers: If you're the lone writer, go to it. This part of the process is yours. If several writers are involved, break the project down into sections to assign to individuals. Another option is to choose someone to write a draft for group review.

Delegator: Make sure team members are clear on deadlines, roles, and responsibilities.

Step 6: Editing the draft

Writer: Before giving your work to the editor, do your own Step 6 edit of the document using the *"Be Your Own Editor" Checklist* on p. 69. Sharing the draft with a peer may also produce some helpful comments. Get distance so that you can review the draft with a more objective eye. While you reread your draft, think about how your team members or reviewers will react. What will they like or dislike? Do their possible reactions suggest changes you could make?

Editor: Use the *"Be Your Own Editor" Checklist* on p. 69 before sending the document "upstairs" to the delegator. If the draft goes through several rounds of edits, use the track-changes feature of your word-processing program to show who makes the changes, where, and when.

How to critique supportively

If you have several people who write for you, you probably prefer the one whose writing gets your signature on first reading. That's the independent writer! Your job as a delegator or editor is to move all of your writers to that level of independence by critiquing them supportively. However, many editors unwittingly create dependence by correcting their writers' errors rather than teaching them to identify and repair their own.

Viewing your job as one of coach rather than editor will help you to encourage independence. Support writers to be their own editors by *commenting* on errors rather than fixing them. If you do all the editing yourself, writers will be less inclined to present their best work to you. Why should they, when they assume you'll change it anyway?

Some typical comments

Instead of revising a paragraph, write in the margin, "Is your most important point in the best place? Please resequence." Point out the errors covered in Part 5, "Quiz Yourself." If you write "dangling modifier" or "passive voice," then writers can refer to "Quiz Yourself" for an explanation of their errors.

Questions are especially helpful because they get writers to think for themselves:

- "Have you used enough headlines?"
- "Will the reader get the wrong impression here?"
- "What was your intended tone? You sound irritated."

More tips for reviewers

1. Expect writers to critique themselves first. Ask, "How do you think you've done thus far?" Place the initial burden of editing on them—and give them a chance to acknowledge their own possible concerns about the document. This strategy can reduce defensiveness.

For example, if the writer has a chance to say, "I may be taking too long to get to the point," the editor can respond, "Well, let's work together on that one." This sets a much more supportive tone for the conversation and makes a writer feel helped rather than criticized by the editor's written comments.

2. Watch your timing. Use good judgment in returning your comments, no matter how nondefensive the writer seems to be. No one likes even a supportive critique after receiving some bad news from another side of life.

3. Show models of reports or proposals to illustrate format as well as style. Examples speak much more clearly than a generalized explanation. Be as specific as you can to help writers understand their goals.

4. Say something positive. Even a beginner's work will have something to commend it. "It's brief and to the point," "Your opener is just what GigaTrix will want to hear," or "You've made a good start" will set a positive tone for the most problem-filled discussions.

When you're writing comments, try to offer at least one positive tidbit for each page you read. People are less defensive when they know you've appreciated their strengths, even if your job is to help them find their weaknesses. Let writers know where they stand with comments like this: "Your proposal is progressing well. To make it a home run, please . . ."

Give as much positive feedback as you can. We hear writers complain that even when their work is perfect, they get nothing but a signature. It can be demoralizing to spend time perfecting a document, never to bask in the success of the project.

5. Comment on the writing, not the writer. People naturally feel vulnerable when they submit their writing to someone else. Try to make it clear from your tone that your comments are not personal attacks; you are focusing on what you see on the page.

Your comments on a written document should meet the same standards for tone that we recommend in our editing discussion in Part 1, Step 6. Be positive, direct, and personable. Judgmental comments such as "fuzzy thinking" cross the line into criticizing writers rather than their word choice. "Please use more precise words to express your point clearly" is much better.

6. Pay attention to the emotional component. Even when the Six Step process seems to be going smoothly, there may be some ruffled feathers. If you suspect unresolved issues, communicate more by asking questions. Often bad feelings stem from insensitivity to others; learning more about their feelings can help you improve the process for the rest of the project.

Case histories: how to avoid team conflict

The two case studies that follow show how miscommunications occur during a team-writing project. The what-went-wrong analysis for each one shows how applying the Six Steps can resolve or prevent such problems. The result is greater productivity, too.

Case History #1: Writing an audit report

The delegator assigns a solo writer

Several months ago, Linda, a specialist in I.T. security, transferred from a supervisory position in the I.T. department to a staff position in the internal-audit department. After her initial training, Linda was assigned to a team investigating possible unauthorized access to highly confidential corporate-personnel files.

Her manager, Peter, established the customary six-week schedule for completing the report because he considered this audit a routine matter. After her initial fact gathering, Linda had trouble organizing many sections. One week before the deadline, Peter was far from pleased with Linda's draft.

Two Points of View	
Linda's	**Peter's**
I'm doing my best, but he keeps sending it back for revisions.	She has all the facts here, but they're hard to follow. Her ideas are all over the place.
If he'd just tell me what he wants, I'd be able to change it. He isn't explaining what I've done wrong.	I don't know where to begin editing her writing. I wish I didn't have to do her work for her.
Why should I work so hard to perfect this? The team says he'll only rewrite my material himself anyway.	We're wasting too much time on all these revisions. I might as well rewrite it myself and get it over with.

What went wrong?

1. Right from the start, there were problems with clarification and communication. Linda didn't ask enough questions. She should have sought more direction when she felt stymied in the first place. Later, to avoid repeating her mistakes, she needed to understand why her manager corrected her work.

   Peter, on the other hand, failed to offer the kind of preliminary direction that would have launched Linda on the project with the information and confidence she needed to write a good report. Note that both members of the team shared responsibility for the communication problem; either one could have improved the situation during the process. Whenever such misunderstandings develop, seldom is only one person to blame.

2. Peter found himself criticizing the organization of Linda's report after she had invested significant time writing her first draft. If they had used an Idea Draft, Peter could have spotted and corrected Linda's Step 3 sequencing problems before she wrote the draft. Now they are faced with the painful prospect of redoing her work.

3. Peter took over too much of the Step 6 editing. Rather than coaching Linda to produce a report appropriate for the internal-audit department, he revised her work himself, giving Linda less incentive to work on her own writing skills. Nor did he explain his edits so she could learn from his suggestions. No wonder they were both frustrated. As we frequently hear from managers, Peter was ready to give up and write it all himself.

Case History #2: Writing a management consulting proposal

The delegator assigns a group of three to write

With an unusually tight deadline for a consulting proposal, Carla assigned her three top financial-management consultants to write different segments. Jane and Terry had worked together before, but Tim was new to the group. Carla had heard he was a good writer.

When Jane and Terry submitted their proposal segments the day before the deadline, Carla was delighted. It was obvious they had collaborated as usual—reviewing each other's writing before sending it to her. Tim's came in the next morning as she was rushing to a meeting. Although the content was excellent in every detail, the writing style was completely different from the one that usually went out of her department. Irritated, Carla sent the segment back to Tim with a one-line note asking him to change his section as soon as possible to conform with the style Jane and Terry used.

Two Points of View

Tim's	Carla's
This is outrageous—there's nothing wrong with this! She might at least have had the courtesy to tell me in advance that she wanted to homogenize me—like everyone else in her group.	I know how hard Tim worked, but his style just doesn't match. I hate to stifle his individuality, but anything that goes out over my signature must have a consistent style throughout. That's what our clients expect.
If that's what I get for taking the trouble to perfect my segment, I'll just send in the rough draft from now on.	I'm sure that after this project, Tim will be able to submit even higher-quality work.

What went wrong?

1. In a classic Step 6 error, the delegator did not instruct the writing team to complete a self-review before handing in their individual sections. If Jane, Terry, and Tim had worked together to edit one another's segments, or if Carla had appointed an editor, they would have spotted the style difference right away. Perhaps the writers could have resolved it themselves, and Tim would have had the benefit of Jane and Terry's experience. Carla should have realized that a new team member, no matter how good a writer, would not be familiar with department standards and style.

2. Carla needs to critique more supportively. All Tim heard was that his style was all wrong; he didn't realize how much his manager appreciated the quality of his work. As a result, Carla has damaged their working relationship. She may not see that quality of writing from Tim again.

3. Being a good writer wasn't enough to ensure that Tim would succeed. Carla failed to communicate her particular expectations. If she had given Tim a sample proposal reflecting her desired style, she could have prevented ill will and finished the proposal without last-minute stress.

More tools to help you

The *Instant-Answer Guide to Business Writing* by Deborah Dumaine has several tools that will help you and your team plan, communicate, and write productively:

1. "Writing as a Team: Suggested Roles" is a guide to assigning roles to team members during each step of the writing process.
2. The "Team-Writing Project Planning Chart" uses the Six Steps to document the team's progress.
3. "How to Edit Constructively" and the "Constructive Editing Comments Guide" will help you point out writing problems to your writers in a positive way.

These tools will help you control the group dynamics that affect the writing process. Use the techniques and strategies you've read in this section to produce a document that drives action. We don't write in a vacuum—we write for readers and sometimes *with* other writers.

Give Meaning to Minutes

As the official record of meetings, minutes have two primary purposes:

- to document decisions: actions planned and deliverables
- to document work assignments: tasks, responsible individuals, and deadlines.

Once approved, minutes can even serve as evidence in a court of law. Therefore, they must be accurate, complete, and clear.

Good minutes spur action

Many a meeting has ended with participants feeling that much was accomplished, only to find later that no one took action on the decisions. The following suggestions are designed to help you write minutes that get results.

Minute-by-minute guidelines

Compare the before-and-after examples on the next page. The "after" minutes clearly reflect the decisions made and the persons responsible for taking action. They also show that the meeting was businesslike—not a waste of company time. It's much more likely that Alan will get the figures to Joan by the deadline if he receives the second set of minutes.

These are the minutes of the meeting held in the Pearson Conference Room on January 9, 2020. Joan, Alan, Steve, and Ida met to discuss how holiday sales went and to talk about how to be better prepared next year. We decided that we just didn't have enough information to discuss things fairly, so we will discuss the topic again in February.

AFTER

Date	January 9, 2020
Purpose of meeting	To evaluate holiday sales
Attendees	Joan C. Crimmons — Sales Manager Alan Lakes — Buyer Steven Jengian — Assistant Buyer Ida Crossley — Assistant Buyer
Topic	Overall sales vs. objectives
Discussion	1. Steve distributed the attached summary of sales. 2. Ida feels we need more data from our competitors to see if we really did poorly or if our objectives were just too high, given this year's spending.
Next steps	• **Alan** will get figures from other retail stores in our area to Joan by **January 29.** • **Joan** will put the topic on the February agenda.

The author of the second set of minutes used the following guidelines.

1. Use headlines and a consistent format

People refer to minutes to remind them of discussion outcomes and assignments. Headlines or sidelines help tremendously. If the meeting is held routinely, use a table with a consistent set of headlines people will see each time.

Here is a sample format:

Agenda topic	Discussion/ decisions	Action steps	Deliverables/ outcome	Who's responsible?	Deadline
1. 2. 3.					

One board of directors that met annually for three days used only the headlines "Topic," "Discussion," and "Action." They installed a template on their laptops, and each board member took turns recording the minutes. No one felt overworked, and the minutes were consistent despite the multi-author approach.

2. Include only a summary of the discussion

Include discussion summaries after the table, and key them to the agenda topic they match. A word-for-word account is both unnecessary and inefficient; just recap the major viewpoints. Give people credit for their ideas, but make sure you don't editorialize or misreport. Avoid judgmental comments like "she interrupted," "they argued," or "he insisted."

3. Provide necessary details only, but do be specific

The room you met in probably isn't relevant. However, if a major decision is being considered, include all debates and outcomes from the discussion. Vagueness wastes time and will make your minutes less valuable.

4. Use a professional yet personable tone

You have to be sensitive to the style and culture of your own organization or the group of people meeting. Sometimes humor is called for, sometimes it's not. One creative minute-taker added a "Weather" headline so he could note, "Rain, finally." He worked for an agriculture-supply house.

5. List complete names and titles

These details take very little extra space. In three years, no one may remember who Joan, Alan, Steve, and Ida were.

6. Highlight action items and deadlines

These are vital to the document. Clearly presented action items guarantee that attendees understand their commitments and the actions expected of them. Well-written minutes assure them that their meeting time was well spent.

Remember, headlines make for easy reference

If you need to refer to minutes six months from now, you won't have to read every word to find the information you need. The headlines will save everyone precious time.

Shape Performance Through Your Writing

Necessary as it is, one of the less pleasant aspects of being a manager is documenting substandard performance by employees.

The scattershot approach

Too often when managers have a gripe about something, they send a corrective memo to *every* team member, guilty or not. Although meant to improve a situation, this strategy usually has the opposite effect. The innocent are insulted; the guilty may be unmoved by such subtleties.

If you must use this technique, a strategic opening sentence will help you aim your communication more accurately. For example: "I know that most of you are extremely punctual for meetings, and I appreciate it more than you can imagine. However, a few of you . . ."

The targeted approach

Dealing with specific individuals, although difficult and unpleasant, is better in the long run. The innocent will appreciate your take-charge management style; the one responsible for the problem will get the message. But the direct approach need not be negative or confrontational. Use the following strategy to document your actions and communicate your concerns in a way that encourages the person to improve or change.

How to write a warning

Always start with face-to-face feedback. If an oral warning is unsuccessful, put your concerns in writing to the individual. Here are some tips:

1. Keep your tone neutral, not threatening.
2. Stick to the facts; describe your concerns and give specific examples.
3. Avoid judgmental adjectives.
4. Focus on the undesirable behaviors instead of criticizing the person.
5. Make or repeat an offer to help.
6. Be clear about improvements expected.
7. Give deadlines and other follow-up planned.

Such documents are highly sensitive. A letter or memo is far more confidential a method of transmission than an e-mail.

Trigger a Response by Letter

It was so simple. In your mind you knew clearly what you wanted to ask, so you sat down and wrote a letter. Simple—except that the response you received seemed to be written to someone else. Maybe you weren't as clear as you thought. We have chosen a simple example to illustrate solutions that you will be able to apply to the most sophisticated situations.

An anxious corporate consumer wrote the letter on the next page. His new purchase was damaged, and he was trying to get it fixed under the provisions of a company warranty. If you were a customer-relations representative of the Euripides Paper Shredder Company, wouldn't you have been confused by this letter?

September 19, 2020

The Euripides Paper Shredder Company
Customer Relations
11540 Columbus Roadway
Melrose, ID 30957

Dear Customer Relations Supervisor:

I am enclosing one of the broken parts from our new paper shredder. The other part that was broken (it had a yellow extension with a red handle) was thrown out by my assistant, who got sick of it sitting on his desk while I was busy looking for your warranty. The red handle was broken right in two.

I really appreciate your guarantee to replace broken parts. And I hope that you will make an allowance for my assistant's having thrown out the other broken part instead of understanding that we had to save it.

Thank you very much.

Sincerely,

Don Savel

Don Savel

Don's letter has several problems, chief among them that he never states clearly what he wants the reader to do. Even though it took him only a couple of minutes to dash his letter off, each follow-up letter that he writes to explain the previous one will take twice as long.

How to get action

Here are several strategies that will ensure a positive response from your letters and save you from Don's dilemma:

- Include a subject line. If you can do it succinctly, state your request in the subject line as well as in the body of the letter.
- Begin with your real purpose. Rarely are enclosures or attachments your most important point, so don't begin with them.
- Choose a tone appropriate to the situation. Avoid angry or sarcastic remarks if you're writing a complaint. They will only alienate your reader—not a very persuasive strategy.
- Express your positive expectations for cooperation. A friendly word or two always helps.
- Supply only enough background material to orient the reader to the situation. Don't obscure your request.
- Before you close, be sure your reader knows what to do. Request specific action: what, when, how. Use headlines such as "Action requested," "Deadlines," and "Next steps."

How will your reader react?

Now, pretend that you are Don Savel, and you just purchased the shredder only to find that two parts were broken. How would you notify the Euripides Paper Shredder Company of your misfortune so that you get your desired action—the replacement of the two damaged parts? Try writing a better version. Here's a chance to use the Six Steps to Reader-Centered Writing.

How did you do?

The "after" letter on p. 212 is our approach. How does your letter compare?

September 19, 2020

The Euripides Paper Shredder Company
Customer Relations
11540 Columbus Roadway
Melrose, ID 30957

Subject: Please replace shredder parts damaged in shipping

Dear Customer Relations Supervisor:

Shredder arrived damaged
Two days ago, I received a new paper shredder, Model #92131X, manufactured by your company. Unfortunately the shredder arrived with two broken parts. I am sure that you will replace the two damaged parts as soon as possible, as your warranty and your reputation promise.

Broken part enclosed
Only one of the broken parts is enclosed. The other, a yellow piece with a red handle attached, was accidentally thrown away. Please accept my word that the second part was broken when I unpacked it.

Please send replacement parts by October 5
I would appreciate your speedy action in delivering the two replacement parts to me. Contact me if you have any questions. Please call me if you can't deliver the parts by October 5.

Thank you for your help.

Sincerely,

Don Savel

Don Savel

Let's examine the contents of each letter, starting with Don's original effort. Do you think the reader had these secret thoughts?

"Before" letter content	Reader's reaction
1. One broken part of the new desktop paper shredder is enclosed.	Unclear explanation.
2. Assistant threw out the other part.	Who cares who did it?
3. I almost lost your warranty.	What an incompetent.
4. I like your guarantee to replace broken parts.	But do you want new parts?

Now let's look at the likely reader response to the second letter.

"After" letter content	Reader's reaction
1. I have a broken paper shredder made by your company.	Aha, I see the problem right away.
2. It came with two broken parts.	Thanks for the exact details.
3. . . . a yellow piece with a red handle attached . . .	Parts described as accurately as possible.
4. Your warranty promises to replace them.	Clear expectations.
5. Please deliver two replacement parts.	I see what you want.
6. Needed by October 5.	I'll see if I can get them in tomorrow's shipments.
7. Any questions, please contact me.	Responsiveness/note of warmth.

I'm sure you'll agree that Don would have saved himself time and achieved the results he sought if he had begun by defining his purpose in writing, outlined his response, and gathered and sequenced all the information he needed *before* he wrote his letter. An edit before sending it would have eliminated the unclear requests and embarrassing self-portrayal.

PART FIVE

Quiz Yourself: Find Your Personal Strengths and Weaknesses

The best effect of any book is that it excites the reader to self-activity.

—THOMAS CARLYLE

In Step 6 we covered the critical editing skills you must apply after you've written your first draft. However, we only briefly mentioned the basic grammar skills. You must also spot and correct those errors as you follow the *"Be Your Own Editor" Checklist.* Although this is not a grammar book, we have included the following quizzes to help you spot your weak points.

Do you need a refresher?

Most of us have a working knowledge of grammar even if we can't remember the rules. To test your grammar skills and your punctuation, try the following grammar quizzes. Do the extra practice exercises if your score shows you need it. Then, to test yourself on the editing skills we discussed in Step 6, go on to "Editing: Quiz Yourself," and the practice exercises.

For more guidance on all issues of grammar, punctuation, and editing, consult our companion volume, the *Instant-Answer Guide to Business Writing: An A–Z Source for Today's Business Writer* by Deborah Dumaine and the Better Communications® Team.

Grammar:
Quiz Yourself

The miniquizzes on the following pages will help you determine your strengths and weaknesses in grammar and punctuation. Each section begins with a quiz. If your score is perfect, go on to the next exercise. If you score below 100 percent, continue by reading the instructions and doing the practice exercise.

See Appendix A for solutions to practice exercises.

Dangling modifiers

Quiz yourself

Decide whether each sentence is correct or incorrect. Check the appropriate box.

	CORRECT	INCORRECT
1. Less expensive, we propose the second option.	❑	❑
2. Closing out the year end, a calculation error jumped out at him.	❑	❑
3. Although he is only an assistant vice president, his parking space is closest to the front entrance.	❑	❑
4. While Director of Communications, several pioneering ideas became realities.	❑	❑

Scoring: 100%: Reward—go on to the quiz on parallelism. Less than 100%: Read the following guideline and complete the practice exercise.

Guideline: Avoid dangling modifiers—phrases that do not logically or clearly modify a specific noun or pronoun. When you can't tell whom or what the introductory word group refers to, rearrange or add to the sentence to include the proper information. *Hint:* Pay special attention to the word directly after the comma. Does it belong there?

Example:

>Packed in Styrofoam, you can ship the Fogg smoke detector anywhere.

Written this way, the sentence means that *you* are packed in Styrofoam, not the detector. Here are two ways to correct this dangling modifier.

Solution #1:

Add the missing subject (Fogg smoke detector) to the beginning of the main statement.

>Packed in Styrofoam, the Fogg smoke detector can be shipped anywhere.

Solution #2:

Add the subject (Fogg smoke detector) and a verb to the modifying phrase to make it a clause.

>When the Fogg smoke detector is packed in Styrofoam, you can ship it anywhere.

Practice exercise

Rewrite the sentences that contain dangling modifiers. (Answers are on p. 253.)

1. After spilling the soup at today's luncheon, the new Zappo contract was lost by John.

2. While I was moving the computer, the keyboard fell on my toe.

3. Preparing for the strategic planning meeting, the energy level waned.

4. By editing carefully, a writer can make just a few words hold enormous meaning.

5. After checking my messages, the letter carrier brought the mail, which I read quickly.

6. When 12 years old, her uncle was promoted to vice president of a global corporation.

7. Unless completely rewired, no engineers should handle the Zone A networking equipment.

8. Our curiosity was aroused, seeing a large gathering of emergency vehicles in the parking lot.

9. While circling the airport, my mind was focused on the upcoming meeting.

10. Used for only two weeks, Jim expects to sell his laptop at a good price.

Parallelism

Quiz yourself

Decide whether these sentences are correct or incorrect. Check the appropriate box.

	CORRECT	INCORRECT
1. The damage was worse than they had anticipated: the rugs were stained, flood damage, and some wiring had to be replaced.	❏	❏
2. Her skills for the new job included researching, organization, and writing of long reports.	❏	❏
3. His prospective employer required five references, but he had only four, so he was worried about his chances of obtaining the job.	❏	❏
4. The personnel department couldn't decide between rental and buying a third copy machine for the upcoming rush.	❏	❏

Scoring: 100%: Reward—go on to the quiz on consistency. Less than 100%: Read the guideline and complete the practice exercise.

Guideline: In a sentence or a list, present parallel ideas in parallel form. In other words, sentence elements with identical functions should have identical construction. To achieve this harmony and equality of ideas, choose one form of a word, phrase, or clause and stick to it. Why? Parallel sentence elements channel the reader's attention in the same way as the refrain in a song—there's a familiar repetition to anticipate.

Example:

His typing is fast and he does it accurately.

Solution:

His typing is fast and accurate.

Practice exercise

In the following sentences, correct the errors in parallelism. Mark "Correct" if the sentence is already correct. (Answers are on p. 253.)

1. The agenda for the meeting is as follows:

    a. calling the meeting to order   c. taking the roll call

    b. set date for next meeting   d. electing new officers.

2. The safety committee voted

    • to install lighting in the parking areas

    • to replace handrails on the stairway

    • that faulty electrical outlets should be replaced

    • to improve clearing ice from the walks.

3. We think she is dedicated and resourceful, and we recommend her for the job.

4. When you make the list, arrange the items in order of importance, write them in parallel form, and all the items should be numbered.

5. Not only was the report disorganized and incomplete, but she misspelled many words.

6. He broke down on the highway, missed the meeting, and lost his cell phone, all in the same day.

7. He is efficient, thorough, and has a lot of imagination in his work.

8. By next Monday, please complete the survey, analyze the results, and you should hand in your report.

9. He enjoyed his new job for many reasons: the challenge, the salary, and it was a good working environment.

10. To conserve energy, follow this procedure when you leave the office:

    a. Check that all electrical equipment has been turned off.

    b. Make sure all windows are closed.

    c. Are any lights left on?

Consistency

Quiz yourself

Are the following sentences correct or incorrect? Check the appropriate box.

	CORRECT	INCORRECT
1. Sometimes a person gives short shrift to exercise because they don't know how to fit it into a busy schedule.	❏	❏
2. It was the third time that the team rejected her proposal. Finally, she falls into her chair, defeated before the next meeting begins. How long could she go on this way?	❏	❏
3. The office needed not only a long table for conferences, but also a new filing cabinet and a place to store old correspondence.	❏	❏
4. Is it possible that the Internet is a disruptive force in society? Do they keep us from reading books and newspapers and communicating with our families, traditionally the primary sources for obtaining information?	❏	❏

ANSWERS:

1. Incorrect: Sometimes people give/because they don't. 2. Incorrect: fell into/meeting began. 3. Correct. 4. Incorrect: Does it keep us.

Scoring: 100%: Reward—go on to the quiz on logical comparisons. Less than 100%: Read the guideline and complete the practice exercise.

Guideline: Sentences and paragraphs should be consistent in tense, in agreement of verbs with subjects, and in agreement of pronouns with nouns. Consistency assures a logical progression of ideas and helps the reader follow your meaning.

Examples: Here are three different types of inconsistency: tense, verb-subject, and pronoun. A correct version follows each incorrect sentence.

1. Tense

    Incorrect:
    Today the Director of Training will appoint several new people to the committee. On his list were Kathy, Brad, and Li.

    Correct:
    Today the Director of Training will appoint several new people to the committee. On his list are Kathy, Brad, and Li.

2. Verb-subject

    Incorrect:
    Each of the day-shift employees start at 8:30 A.M.

    Correct:
    Each of the day-shift employees starts at 8:30 A.M.

3. Pronoun

    Incorrect:
    When someone has a cold, they should drink plenty of fluids.

    Correct:
    People with colds should drink plenty of fluids.

Practice Exercise

Find and underline the inconsistencies in the following examples. (Answers are on p. 254.)

1. Sometimes a person cannot decide whether they would rather have a raise or a vacation.

2. The laptop computer is a time-saving, space-saving invention. They are not difficult to use.

3. To change the printer cartridge, first turn off the machine. Open the lid and release the red lever. Do not try to lift out the cartridge until you release the lever. Once the lever was released, the cartridge comes off easily.

4. Arriving late at work is a problem we all have from time to time. Sometimes we are late because family responsibilities conflict with work responsibilities, and you feel caught in the middle.

5. He walked up on the stage, grabbed the microphone, and tells a few hilarious jokes as an icebreaker.

6. Routine tasks we can do almost without thinking. New tasks require greater concentration, but all tasks require attention to detail. Alternating the routine with the new refreshes us and help ensure that our attention to detail never wavers.

7. We developed the new Web site after our two companies merged. They have on-line support and a self-help database.

8. On the day before her vacation, she handed in her report, answered all pending correspondence, and organizes her desk.

9. Concentration is the greater part of any skill. If a person wishes to learn a new skill, they must know how to concentrate.

10. If a reader wants to increase his reading speed, he should begin by examining the entire book or article in question. Once he assimilates the main ideas, he can look at the details. You should strive to master this technique in order to read more quickly.

Logical comparisons

Quiz yourself

Decide whether the following sentences are correct or incorrect. Check the appropriate box.

	CORRECT	INCORRECT
1. The new employee's Spanish was better than many native speakers.	❑	❑
2. He was better prepared for his speech than any other speech I've heard in a long time.	❑	❑

3. The consultant's time-management study proved that our strategy is more efficient than ITT. ❏   ❏

4. This is among the easiest, if not the easiest, quiz I've ever taken. ❏   ❏

Scoring: 100%: Reward—go on to the quiz for pronoun agreement. Less than 100%: Read the guidelines and complete the practice exercise.

Guidelines:

1. When making comparisons, clearly identify the parallels or differences between the things you compare. You can make logical comparisons only between things of the same class.
2. If you want to make two comparisons in the same sentence, be sure to complete the first before starting the second.

Example:

This is one of the best products we manufacture, if not the best.

Practice exercise

The following sentences are ambiguous as they stand. Delete, add, or rearrange words as needed to make logical comparisons. (Answers are on p. 255.)

1. Our policies are different from Lang Realty.

2. Boston Oil's policy on absenteeism is like Acme Industries.

3. Roy is not only one of the most progressive but also dynamic leaders in our region.

4. I know the treasurer better than the general manager.

5. Jim's cash outlay amounted to $50 more than his partner.

6. Roberto plays golf more than his colleagues.

7. Our health benefits are different from our competitor.

8. Sarah's sales report is better organized than her assistant.

9. My office is bigger than my manager.

Pronoun agreement

Quiz yourself

Are these sentences correct or incorrect? Check the appropriate box.

	CORRECT	INCORRECT
1. Ingrid was clearer than me about her choice for president.	❑	❑
2. Between you and I, I feel that the proposal was not fair to minority groups.	❑	❑
3. Us optimists have to stick together.	❑	❑
4. If a person makes a mistake, they should admit it and not hide the truth.	❑	❑

ANSWERS: 1. Incorrect: clearer than I. 2. Incorrect: Between you and me. 3. Incorrect: We optimists. 4. Incorrect: If people make mistakes.

Scoring: 100%: Reward—go on to the quiz on commas. Less than 100%: Read the guidelines and complete the practice exercise.

Guidelines:

1. If a pronoun replaces or functions as the subject of a clause or sentence, use

Singular	Plural
I	we
you	you
he, she, it	they

Example:

> The devil made me do it.   He made me do it.

2. If a pronoun replaces or functions as the object of a verb or preposition, use:

Singular	Plural
me	us
you	you
him, her, it	them

Examples:

> The memo praised Brian.   The memo praised him.
>
> Send the letter to Sally and Greg.   Send the letter to her and Greg.

Remember: Before choosing a pronoun, determine how you will use it in the sentence. Also decide whether the pronoun is replacing a single or plural noun or nouns.

Practice exercise

Think carefully about the function of each pronoun in the sentences below. Circle the correct form. (Answers are on p. 255.)

1. Between you and (I, me), the company seems on the edge of bankruptcy.

2. Two consultants, Dale and (he, him), made the decision.

3. (We, Us) architects must consider beauty as well as strength in our designs.

4. He showed (we, us) newcomers the training video.

5. Hal was more irritated about the invoice than (I, me).

6. (She, Her) and (me, I) were the only ones who could have done the job.

7. If we need to brainstorm, I'd like to include (he, him) and Tim.

8. Among (us, we) executives at the conference, there were many from Chicago.

9. Alice and (she, her) wrote the speech.

10. The award for the best speech of the year went to Alice and (she, her).

Commas

Quiz yourself

Which sentences require commas? Supply the missing commas where needed.

1. Steven Marx who has a melodious voice is very effective on the telephone.

2. The office that he works in is spacious.

3. Anyone with Web-development skills has an edge in today's job market.

4. He will take advice from any person he considers knowledgeable.

5. This system which has been tested in 25 major office buildings across the country is infallible.

Scoring: 100%: Reward—go on to the quiz for semicolons. Less than 100%: Read the guideline and complete the practice exercise.

Guideline: Use commas before and after phrases or clauses when the information in them offers added facts about the subject. If the phrase could be omitted because it isn't essential to the meaning of the sentence, use commas to set it off.

Example:

Peter Schreiber, who began his career in electrical engineering, is the owner of the firm.

Solution:

The clause "who began his career in electrical engineering" is an added fact about Peter Schreiber. You could omit it and not alter the meaning of the sentence. Therefore, use commas.

Example:

All employees who work this Sunday will be paid overtime.

Solution:

The clause "who work this Sunday" could not be omitted. It is essential to the meaning of the sentence because it identifies *which* employees. Therefore, do not use commas.

Practice exercise

Supply the missing commas where needed. (Answers are on p. 255.)

1. Our company which employs 1,800 people is the largest manufacturer in the area.

2. The men and women who work in management are well motivated.

3. People will usually try harder for a manager whom they consider fair.

4. The earth which has a limited amount of fossil-fuel resources can support only a finite number of people and their homes, cars, planes, and offices.

5. Any person who is as intelligent as Donna can have a job with the firm.

6. I have never known a manager who was as efficient as Frank.

7. Tanya Brock who has never missed a day of work was promoted yesterday.

8. I believe that a firm should not manufacture any product that is useless to society.

9. This desk which is an antique is his pride and joy.

10. Often the people who are the loudest have the least to say.

Semicolons

Quiz yourself

Are these sentences correct or incorrect? Check the appropriate box.

	CORRECT	INCORRECT
1. The department's trip to the Ice Follies was canceled; because of the bad storm and the warning of local authorities to stay off the roads.	❏	❏
2. The document is a fake, we found the real one in the president's office.	❏	❏

3. Our new equipment takes up a lot of office space,   ❑   ❑
   consequently, we must now rearrange the furniture.

4. Working in the training department was a wise choice for
   Nancy; she is a natural with people.   ❑   ❑

ANSWERS:

1. Incorrect (no semicolon).   2. Incorrect: *fake; we found.*   3. Incorrect: *space;*   *consequently,*   4. Correct.

Scoring: 100%: Reward—go on to the quiz on colons. Less than 100%: Read the guidelines and complete the practice exercise.

Guidelines:

1. Use a semicolon to link two closely related complete sentences. Independent clauses must always precede and follow a semicolon.

Example:

> We cannot predict how long the study will take; we have never conducted this type of analysis before.

2. Use a semicolon to precede independent clauses that begin with transition words such as *however, moreover, therefore, consequently,* or *for example.*

Example:

> This training manual is confusing; moreover, it lacks an index and a table of contents.

3. Use a semicolon to separate items in a list or series when any of those items contains a comma.

Example:

> The three people authorized to sign checks are Vincent Cabral, the president; Dora Bidiak, the treasurer; and Leslie Trawler, the office manager.

Practice exercise

Insert a semicolon in the following sentences where required. (Answers are on p. 256.)

---

1. Procrastination can derail a project deadline we must all learn to recognize it.

2. The department needs the new equipment, however, there is no room to install it.

3. We'd like everyone to contribute something to the staff party for example, bring cheese, crackers, cider, soda, cake, or cookies.

4. When I'm on time, no one notices when I'm late, the whole office knows.

5. The telephone survey showed that the bank's services were little known consequently, the PR department started a new publicity campaign.

6. The managers had planned to discontinue that service however, an overwhelming customer demand persuaded them to retain it.

7. We enjoyed our visit to the desktop-publishing department moreover, we were glad to meet the staff.

8. We are tightening security therefore, we will not issue night passes this year.

9. She dislikes committee work consequently, she declined the position.

10. If you need more exercise, don't use the elevator take the stairs.

11. We would like to give him a farewell party however, he would prefer that we do not.

12. We cannot meet this deadline we would like an extension.

13. He opened my mail for me while I was on vacation he even answered most of my letters.

14. The job carries several diverse responsibilities for example, you must prepare the budget, design and implement new systems, and oversee a staff of six.

15. We have several choices, all of them interesting.

16. The company softball team lost two out of three games this summer, but morale remained high.

Colons

Quiz yourself

Which of these sentences are punctuated correctly? Check the appropriate box.

		CORRECT	INCORRECT

1. Marianne is brilliant in her field: artificial intelligence. ❑ ❑

2. We need to order the following; 500 letterheads, 500 envelopes, 1,000 address labels, and 3 reams of printer paper. ❑ ❑

3. Whoever reserves a booth early for the expo receives a discount: one way to minimize costs. ❑ ❑

4. Dear Monica, ❑ ❑

Scoring: 100%: Reward—go on to the quiz on dashes. Less than 100%: Read the guidelines and complete the practice exercise.

Guidelines:

1. Use a colon after a name in the salutation of a business letter.

Examples:

Dear Ms. Culpepper:
Dear Martin:

2. Use a colon to link a list or series to its connecting thought.

Example:

Six states are participating in the conference: New Jersey, Oklahoma, New York, Florida, Texas, and California.

3. It is incorrect to use a colon after a preposition or after a form of the verb *to be*.

Examples:

Distribute these forms to human resources, finance, sales, and I.T.
The departments that need these forms are human resources, finance, sales, and I.T.
The following departments need these forms: human resources, finance, sales, and I.T.

4. Use a colon to introduce an amplification of a statement or idea. When used this way, the colon replaces such words as *that is, namely,* or *for example.*

Example:

>   There is only one way to do things: the right way.

Practice exercise

>   Decide where colons should replace commas. (Answers are on p. 256.)

>   1. Make an outline, headline each paragraph, begin each paragraph with a topic sentence, and proofread for spelling and punctuation.

>   2. Several of our functions were outsourced within the last few years, technical support, payroll, and shipping.

>   3. The nurse gave him the same old advice, drink plenty of liquids, get lots of rest, and take vitamin C.

>   4. We have three salespeople in each of our four regions the Northeast, the Mid-Atlantic states, the Northwest, the Southwest.

>   5. The board met in January but could not take a vote, the chair, the secretary, the treasurer, and two members were absent with the flu.

>   6. There is only one thing to dispel the midwinter gloom in this office, a party.

>   7. Vacation time increases with length of service, one week the first year, two weeks the second through the fifth year, three weeks thereafter.

>   8. I cannot begin without the following equipment, a laptop with expanded memory, a scanner, a color printer, a CD burner.

>   9. We all know why business is booming, Christmas is a week away.

>   10. Dear Fred,

Dashes

Quiz yourself

Which sentences are punctuated correctly? Check the appropriate box.

	CORRECT	INCORRECT
1. Formal words can make you sound insecure—something no manager can afford.	❏	❏

2. The book begins with the simplest writing task—a short letter   ❑   ❑
   or e-mail—and then moves on to more challenging issues.

3. Please wait—until I complete the section on nanotechnology.   ❑   ❑

4. Her eyes kept returning to the screen—the blank screen.   ❑   ❑

> **ANSWERS:**
> 1. Correct. 2. Correct. 3. Incorrect (no dash). 4. Correct.

Scoring: 100%: Reward—go on to the quiz on apostrophes. Less than 100%: Read the guidelines and complete the practice exercise.

Guidelines:

1. Use a dash to indicate an emphatic pause.

Example:

> He knew he had closed the sale—they asked for a contract.

2. Use a dash to repeat an idea for emphasis.

Example:

> The office was cold—ice-cold.

3. Use dashes to set off an explanatory expression that needs emphasis.

Example:

> The chip—which consumes only 100 mW—quickly converts text into speech.

Practice exercise

Decide whether a dash could improve the following sentences. Some are correct either way. (Answers are on p. 257.)

1. The suburban branch will be closed by the end of this month, unless its sales pick up unexpectedly.

2. He designed, produced, and distributed the posters you saw around the building.

3. Only one system, the XR70, can perform all the functions listed here.

4. The manager was new to the firm, brand-new.

5. If I were you, and I'm glad I'm not, I'd rewrite the report.

6. All our employees, overseas staff included, are eligible for the profit-sharing plan after two years' consecutive service.

7. I gave many specific examples, all well documented. Still, no one understood the problem.

8. Please visit our new showrooms, the new models have arrived.

9. If this trend continues, and there is no reason why it should not, we will show unprecedented profits this year.

10. You are the last one included in our retirement plan; you signed up just in time.

Apostrophes

Quiz yourself

Which sentences are correct? Check the appropriate box.

	CORRECT	INCORRECT
1. When the package arrived in the mailroom, we were mystified by it's contents.	❏	❏
2. Look what she has accomplished in only two years time.	❏	❏
3. Genes happiness with the job was a pleasure to see, and his enthusiasm was contagious.	❏	❏
4. Please use the rear entrance in the evening; its the only one open after 6 P.M.	❏	❏

ANSWERS:
1. Incorrect: *its.*   2. Incorrect: *years'.*   3. Incorrect: *Gene's.*   4. Incorrect: *it's.*

Scoring: 100%: Go on to "Editing: Quiz Yourself." Less than 100%: Read the guidelines and complete the practice exercise.

Guidelines:

1. Form the possessive of a singular noun or a plural noun not ending in *s* by adding an apostrophe and an *s*. Form the possessive of a plural noun ending in *s* by adding only the apostrophe—for example, "a managers' meeting," "the two technicians' findings."

2. Also use the apostrophe alone to form the possessive of plurals ending in *es,* as in "the witnesses' testimony."

3. Apostrophes have traditionally been used to form the plural of letters and numbers ("mind your p's and q's"), but the more recent approach is to drop apostrophes whenever the meaning will not be affected—for example, "1990s" or "CD-ROMs." Always add both an apostrophe and an *s* to form the singular possessive, however ("the YMHA's building fund").

Practice exercise

The following sentences need apostrophes. Put the 18 missing apostrophes where they belong. (Answers are on p. 257.)

1. His planner always seems to end up on Miles desk.

2. Fridays sales meeting was canceled on account of Chris Jones illness.

3. The new assistants job is to proofread all of the defending lawyers and the prosecuting attorneys briefs before the trials.

4. Smith & Dawsons system is the same model as Royal Regions.

5. Jims insistence that he can't work with Mary makes the offices atmosphere tense.

6. Womens retirement needs are different from mens because statistically they live longer.

7. Sudden power surges can damage a computers drives and circuit boards.

8. The PCs backup system isn't working.

9. He thought Sarahs reports were more carefully researched than either Dawns or his.

10. The X2000s cost is greater than the X1000s, which was developed in the 1990s.

Editing: Quiz Yourself

The following quizzes, guidelines, and practice exercises supplement the editing skills explained in Step 6 of Reader-Centered Writing®. If you need more practice, go back to Step 6 and study the related sections there.

Streamlined sentences

Quiz yourself

Decide whether each sentence needs streamlining. Check the appropriate box.

	YES	NO
1. The critical factor here is to make sure that all the machines that are heavily used are checked not fewer than two times a year.	❏	❏
2. The information provided in this accounting seminar can only make improvements in my future accounting assignments required for the job.	❏	❏
3. He has accomplished the development of many excellent computer programs for more than one company, which therefore seems to have given him the experience and knowledge of the skills necessary to succeed in this position.	❏	❏

4. Our requirement is to make available the ability to prepare ☐ ☐
   several versions of expense units based on probable variations.

ANSWERS:

1.Yes: It is critical to check all heavily used machines at least twice a year.   2.Yes: This accounting seminar can only improve my future on-the-job assignments.   3.Yes: He has developed many excellent computer programs for companies, so he has the experience and skill to succeed in this position.   4.Yes: We must be able to prepare several versions of expense units based on probable variations.

Scoring: 100%: Reward—go on to the quiz for the active voice. Less than 100%: Read the guideline and complete the practice exercise.

Guideline: To prevent wordiness, ask yourself, "What is my message here?" Weed out any words or phrases that do not contribute to the reader's understanding. Use a single word to summarize a group of words; for example, *now* easily replaces *at this point in time.*

Practice exercise

Streamline the following sentences by omitting or changing unnecessary words or phrases, rearranging sections, or dividing sentences. (Answers are on p. 257.)

1. I certainly appreciated the chance to have the opportunity to meet with you and Arthur Forbes for lunch today, and I hope that you found our discussion to be worthwhile.

2. This letter is just a note to be sure that you and I understand what you said would be the criteria for determining the qualifications we are looking for in a new programmer for Section B.

3. What I have done is read every one of the invoices in question and pulled all the ones that I think we should have the bookkeeper look at.

4. I have a meeting scheduled with Gretchen on Monday to go over our fees and a few of the new requirements that some companies are asking me for.

5. Enclosed you will find various selected pages from the draft volume of the analysis guide that is being developed to help assist operators in the implementation of the new form of software.

6. As a result of a recent meeting I just had with Human Resources, I feel it is warranted that I recommend the hiring of Fred Brown for the position of Security Guard, which he seems well qualified for.

7. The reason for the computer blowup yesterday is really that the error file has been increasing daily, and yesterday was the day that it went over 100 items.

8. In the unusual event that we might want to make an adjustment to the totals for any reason on the following day, we can make the needed adjustment by manually altering the figures.

9. You have asked the question as to what our fees would be.

10. If the stock arrives without any identification as to whom it belongs to, it can involve quite a bit of time in tracking it down.

11. I am now in the process of finalizing my draft and plan on spending some time working tonight so that my assistant may have it proofread and delivered to you by noon tomorrow.

12. If there is any further information you need, please do not hesitate to contact me.

Active voice

Quiz yourself

In each pair of sentences, which is better, A or B? Check the appropriate box.

	A	B
1. (A) Many software programs have been adapted to our needs by the I.T. department.	❏	❏
(B) The I.T. department has adapted many software programs to our needs.		
2. (A) The statistics were compiled by Chandra, but the report was written by Simon.	❏	❏
(B) Chandra compiled the statistics, but Simon wrote the report.		
3. (A) You can submit suggestions and comments about this presentation until Friday.	❏	❏
(B) Suggestions and comments can be given about this presentation until Friday.		

	A	B

4. (A) The presentation was delivered to a large audience, and the speaker was animated and persuasive. ☐ ☐

   (B) The speaker, who was animated and persuasive, delivered the presentation to a large audience.

Scoring: 100%: Reward—go on to the quiz on gobbledygook. Less than 100%: Read the guideline and complete the practice exercise.

Guideline: Use the active voice as often as possible. Use the passive voice only when you don't know who is performing the action, the actor is not significant, or you want to avoid naming the person responsible for the action.

Practice exercise

Change the following sentences from the passive to the active voice by rearranging them to show who or what is the actor—the doer of the action. Supply an actor if necessary. (Answers are on p. 258.)

1. Her proposal ought to be given our serious consideration.

2. This conference, as was true also of the last one, was made possible through the outstanding organizing abilities of one person.

3. Confirmation is given by the data concerning the rising rate of turnover in our department.

4. All the lights should be turned off before you leave the office.

5. It is expected that our president will be told that our best client was hopelessly alienated by our new salesperson.

6. An analysis of this toxic substance will be disclosed soon.

7. It has been decided that a time clock will be installed.

8. Variable fields are indicated on the screen by underscores, so that as you enter information, the underscores are replaced by the data that you enter.

9. A decision has to be reached soon, or the contract may be lost.

10. This intolerable situation must be remedied immediately.

Gobbledygook

Quiz yourself

In each pair of sentences, which contains gobbledygook, A or B? Check the appropriate box.

	A	B

1. (A) The company must turn to top-priority tasks to reach its goal. ☐ ☐

   (B) It is now incumbent on the company to prioritize its tasks within the parameters of its goal expectation.

2. (A) Andrea's real skill performance on the job showed a negative correlation with her potential skill performance. ☐ ☐

   (B) Andrea did not do as well in the job as she could have.

3. (A) In answer to your letter of January 26, I am working on a solution that will be mutually satisfactory. ☐ ☐

   (B) Regarding your letter of January 26, which I am now in possession of, I beg your indulgence while I frame a response that does not give preferential treatment to either your company or ours.

4. (A) At the agency, the work-difficulty element involved rendered inoperative their expectation of task completion within the originally prescribed time frame. ☐ ☐

   (B) The agency's work was so difficult that the employees did not finish on time.

ANSWERS: 1. B. 2. A. 3. B. 4. A.

Scoring: 100%: Reward—go on to the quiz on words and tone. Less than 100%: Read the guideline and complete the practice exercise.

Guideline: To avoid gobbledygook, use the simplest, most concise language that will accurately express your ideas.

Practice exercise

Rewrite the following sentences to eliminate gobbledygook. (Answers are on p. 258.)

1. The termination of the product line will facilitate the advancement of the company's overall sales.

2. We would like to ask that you forward your spouse's Social Security number to the firm at your earliest convenience.

3. In view of the fact that the treasurer deems it important to institute a policy terminating managers over age 68, we will peruse his recommendations most seriously.

4. During the course of the week, I have utilized every available source to locate the materials.

5. We are in need of your assistance in ascertaining what has transpired since we first communicated.

6. Your cooperation in obtaining information as to the residences of employees hired prior to 2020 would be appreciated.

7. Did you obtain a copy of Mr. Quibble's communication requesting all personnel to indicate in writing when they intend to make use of a company vehicle?

8. I am contacting you with respect to initiating a stress-management program within the confines of our office building.

9. Did you sustain any mental or physical injuries as a consequence of the accident?

10. We would like to request that you comply with the ensuing directions and complete the attached forms in detail.

Words and tone

Quiz yourself

Choose a less formal word to replace each of the words below.

1. sufficient _____

2. to supply _____

3. to incorporate _____

4. to transpire _____

Scoring 100%: Reward—go on to the quiz on positive approach. Less than 100%: Read the guideline and complete the practice exercise.

Guideline: Don't use an inflated word if a down-to-earth one will do the job as well.

Practice exercise

Fill in each blank using a less formal word with the same meaning. (Answers are on p. 259.)

1. to anticipate _____
2. to apprise _____
3. to ascertain _____
4. to assist _____
5. to concur _____
6. to deem _____
7. to desire _____
8. to determine _____
9. to disclose _____
10. to effect _____
11. to endeavor _____
12. to ensue _____
13. to execute _____
14. to forward _____
15. to furnish _____
16. in as much as _____
17. to indicate _____
18. initially _____
19. in lieu of _____
20. in the event that _____
21. to locate _____
22. to state _____
23. pertaining to _____
24. presently _____
25. prior to _____
26. to prohibit _____
27. to request _____
28. to require _____
29. residence _____
30. to surmise _____

Positive approach

Quiz yourself

Rewrite these sentences in a more positive way.

1. This letter isn't up to our standards.

   _____

2. If you don't improve your attendance record, you won't be promoted.

   _____

3. Without careful preparation, we won't be able to win the account.

   _____

4. It would not be objectionable if you attended the workshop in the fall.

   _____

Scoring: 100%: Reward—go on to "Your Personal Profile Graph." Less than 100%: Read the guideline and complete the practice exercise.

Guideline: Choose words that convey a confident, positive attitude. Avoid unnecessary negatives.

Practice exercise

Rewrite the following sentences in a more positive way. (Answers are on p. 260.)

1. We hope you will not be disappointed with the results.

   _____

2. Without proper planning, we will not be able to prevent overcrowding.

   _____

3. We are sorry, but we cannot process your order until you have paid the balance on your account.

_____

4. If you don't like my suggestions, please contact me.

_____

5. No doubt the changes should prove worthwhile.

_____

6. Do not ignore details; they are important.

_____

7. This job is going to be nearly impossible to do.

_____

Your Personal Profile Graph

Now that you've polished your skills, start applying what you've learned to your daily writing. Editing will be easier if you have a list of your strengths and weaknesses before you. It will remind you to apply actively what you've learned. Use the Personal Profile Graph to map your skills. Then make a list of your weaknesses and post it by your desk for quick reference when editing.

Flip back through the practice exercises in Part 5 and note your strengths and weaknesses in each by calculating your percentage of correct answers. Consider a score of less than 70 percent a weakness. To complete the profile, plot your scores on the following graph. You might also want to post a copy of the graph next to your list of weaknesses.

Personal Profile Graph
Score: % Correct

	10%	20%	30%	40%	50%	60%	70%	80%	90%	100%
Dangling Modifiers										
Parallelism										
Consistency										
Logical Comparisons										
Pronoun Agreement										
Commas										
Semicolons										
Colons										
Dashes										
Apostrophes										
Streamlined Sentences										
Active Voice										
Gobbledygook										
Words and Tone										
Positive Approach										

Action Plan

Now that you've learned processes for writing most types of documents and assessed some of your skills, it's time for you to develop your own plan for putting your new knowledge into action.

Make a list of your intentions for your next writing project. What will you do differently? What are your writing goals?

My Action Plan

1. Writing issue:
   Action step:

2. Writing issue:
   Action step:

3. Writing issue:
   Action step:

4. Writing issue:
   Action step:

Solutions to Exercises

Marketing letter Q&A (from p. 111)

1. The second one.
2. Pompous, insulting, condescending, cold.
3. Friendly, warm, sincere, down-to-earth, the "you" attitude.
4. Her own company.
5. The interests and needs of the potential client.
6. Number 2. It was lively and competent. Goodman sounded like a go-getter.
7. Number 2. She suggests an exact date. Good idea!

Dangling modifiers (from p. 218)

1. After spilling the soup at today's luncheon, John lost the new Zappo contract.
2. Correct.
3. Our energy level waned as we prepared for the strategic planning meeting.
4. Correct.
5. The letter carrier brought the mail, which I read quickly after checking my messages.
6. Her uncle was promoted to vice president of a global corporation when she was 12 years old.
7. Unless the Zone A networking equipment is completely rewired, no engineers should handle it.
8. Our curiosity was aroused after we saw a large gathering of emergency vehicles in the parking lot.
9. While we circled the airport, my mind was focused on the upcoming meeting.
10. Jim expects to sell his laptop, used for only two weeks, at a good price.

Parallelism (from p. 219)

1. a. Correct.
   b. setting the date for the next meeting
   c. Correct.
   d. Correct.

   or

1. a. call the meeting to order.
   b. set the date for the next meeting.
   c. take the roll call.
   d. elect new officers.

2. a. Correct.
   b. Correct.
   c. to replace faulty electrical outlets.
   d. Correct.
3. Correct.
4. When you make the list, arrange the items in order of importance, write them in parallel form, and number them.
5. Her report was not only disorganized and incomplete, but it was also full of misspelled words.
6. Correct.
7. He is efficient, thorough, and imaginative in his work.
8. By next Monday, please complete the survey, analyze the results, and hand in your report.
9. He enjoyed his new job for many reasons: the challenge, the salary, and the working environment.
10. a. Correct.
    b. Correct.
    c. make sure no lights are left on.

Consistency (from p. 221)

1. Sometimes *people* cannot decide whether they would rather have a raise or a vacation.
2. *It* is not difficult to use.
3. *Once you release the lever,* the cartridge comes off easily.
4. Sometimes we are late because family responsibilities conflict with work responsibilities and *we* feel caught in the middle.
5. He walked up on the stage, grabbed the microphone, and *told* a few hilarious jokes as an icebreaker.
6. Alternating the routine with the new refreshes us and *helps* ensure that our attention to detail never wavers.
7. *It has* on-line support and a self-help database.
8. On the day before her vacation, she handed in her report, answered all pending correspondence, and *organized* her desk.
9. If *people wish* to learn a new skill, *they* must know how to concentrate. *Or: Those who wish* to learn a new skill must know how to concentrate.
10. If *readers want* to increase *their* reading speed, *they* should begin by examining the entire book or article in question. Once *they assimilate* the main

ideas, *they* can look at the details. *Readers* should strive to master this technique in order to read more quickly.

Or: If *you want* to increase *your* reading speed, *you* should begin by examining the entire book or article in question. Once *you assimilate* the big ideas, *you* can look at the details. You should strive to master this technique in order to read more quickly.

Logical comparisons (from p. 224)

1. Our policies are different from Lang Realty's (policies).
2. Boston Oil's policy on absenteeism is like Acme Industries (policy).
3. Roy is not only one of the most progressive leaders in our region, he's also the most dynamic.
4. I know the treasurer better than I know the general manager.
5. Jim's cash outlay amounted to $50 more than his partner's (cash outlay).
6. Roberto plays golf more than his colleagues do.
7. Our health benefits are different from our competitor's (health benefits).
8. Sarah's sales report is better organized than her assistant's.
9. My office is bigger than my manager's (office).

Pronoun agreement (from p. 226)

1. me
2. he
3. We
4. us
5. I
6. She, I
7. him
8. us
9. she
10. her

Commas (from p. 228)

1. Our company, which employs 1,800 people, is the largest manufacturer in the area.
2. Correct.

3. Correct.
4. The earth, which has a limited amount of fossil-fuel resources, can support only a finite number of people and their homes, cars, planes, and offices.
5. Correct.
6. Correct.
7. Tanya Brock, who has never missed a day of work, was promoted yesterday.
8. Correct.
9. This desk, which is an antique, is his pride and joy.
10. Correct.

Semicolons (from p. 230)

1. deadline;
2. equipment;
3. party;
4. notices;
5. known;
6. service;
7. department;
8. security;
9. work;
10. elevator;
11. party;
12. deadline;
13. vacation;
14. responsibilities;
15. Correct.
16. Correct.

Colons (from p. 232)

1. Correct.
2. years:*
3. advice:*
4. regions:
5. vote:*
6. office:*

---

*A colon is not the only acceptable solution here—see the section on dashes. In #5, a semicolon, instead of a colon, is also correct.

---

7. service:
8. equipment:
9. booming:
10. Correct.

Dashes (from p. 233)

1. month—unless
2. Correct.
3. system—the XR70—can
4. firm—brand-new
5. you—and I'm glad I'm not—I'd
6. employees—overseas staff included—are
7. examples—all
8. showrooms—the new models
9. continues—and there is no reason why it should not—we
10. plan—you

Apostrophes (from p. 235)

1. Miles's
2. Friday's, Jones's
3. assistant's, lawyers', attorneys'
4. Dawson's, Region's
5. Jim's, office's
6. Women's, men's
7. computer's
8. PC's
9. Sarah's, Dawn's
10. X2000's, 1000's; either 1990s or 1990's is correct (1990s is preferred)

Streamlined sentences (from p. 238)

There are many ways to streamline these sentences. Here are some suggestions:

1. I enjoyed lunch with you and Arthur Forbes today. I hope you found our discussion worthwhile.
2. I want to confirm our criteria for determining the qualifications of a new Section B programmer.

3. I have pulled all the invoices I feel the bookkeeper should review.
4. On Monday, Gretchen and I will meet to discuss our fees and some new company requirements.
5. Enclosed are some pages from the draft of the analysis guide we're developing to help operators implement the new software.
6. After meeting with Human Resources, I recommend Fred Brown for the Security Guard position—he is well qualified.
7. The computer blew up yesterday because the error file went over 100 items.
8. If we want to adjust the totals on the following day, we can do so manually.
9. You asked about our fees.
10. Tracking down unidentified stock can be time-consuming.
11. I'll work on my draft tonight so that you'll have it tomorrow.
12. If you need more information, please contact me.

Active voice (from p. 240)

1. We should give her proposal our serious consideration.
2. One person's outstanding organizing abilities made the conference possible both this year and last.
3. The data confirm the rising turnover rate in our department.
4. Please turn off all lights before you leave the office.
5. We expect someone to tell our president that our new salesperson hopelessly alienated our best client.
6. We will soon disclose an analysis of this toxic substance.
7. Management has decided to install a time clock.
8. The information you enter replaces the underscores that indicate variable fields on the screen.
9. We must reach a decision soon, or we may lose the contract.
10. We must remedy this intolerable situation immediately.

Gobbledygook (from p. 242)

1. Dropping this product line will improve the company's overall sales.
2. Please send the firm your spouse's Social Security number as soon as possible.
3. Because the treasurer feels it is important to start letting go of managers over age 68, we will read his recommendation seriously.
4. This week I asked everybody in the office to help me find the materials.
5. We need your help in order to find out what happened since we first contacted you.

6. Would you please help us find the home addresses of employees hired before 2020?
7. Did you get a copy of Mr. Quibble's memo asking all employees to inform him in writing when they need a company car?
8. Would you be interested in starting a stress-management program in our office building?
9. Were you injured in the accident?
10. Kindly follow the directions and complete the attached forms in detail.

Words and tone (from p. 243)

1. to expect
2. to tell
3. to find out
4. to help
5. to agree with
6. to consider or think
7. to want
8. to find out
9. to tell
10. to cause or bring about
11. to try
12. to follow
13. to do
14. to send
15. to give
16. because
17. to say or show
18. at first
19. instead of
20. if
21. to find
22. to say
23. of or about
24. soon
25. before
26. to forbid or prevent
27. to ask for
28. to need

29. home or address
30. to guess

Positive approach (from p. 244)

1. We're sure you will be pleased with the results.
2. With proper planning, there will be space for everyone.
3. As soon as we receive your payment, we will process your order.
4. If you want to comment on my suggestions, please contact me.
5. We expect the changes to be beneficial.
6. Pay attention to details; they are important.
7. This job is going to be a challenge.

Fry's Readability Graph

Rating Readability Manually

If you don't have a computer program for rating the readability level of your writing, do it by hand. Edward Fry, Ph.D., formerly director of the Reading Center at Rutgers University, designed the Graph for Estimating Readability of documents on p. 264.

Check sentence length and word length

1. Select a 100-word passage. A "word" is defined as a group of symbols with a space on either side. Therefore, *Joe, JRA, 2020,* and *&* are counted as words.

2. Count the number of sentences. Round to the nearest tenth. You may have 7.6 or 8.2 sentences when you include the fraction of the last sentence that isn't finished within the 100-word sample.

3. Count the number of syllables. Syllables are defined phonetically: there are as many syllables as vowel sounds. For example, *stopped* is one syllable and *wanted* is two syllables.

    If each word contained one syllable, you would have 100 syllables. So you can use 100 as a base and count only the syllables in words that have more than one syllable. Tally the figures as follows: one slash mark for a two-syllable word, two slashes for a three-syllable word, etc. Then, count the slashes and add the result to 100.

Graph for Estimating Readability

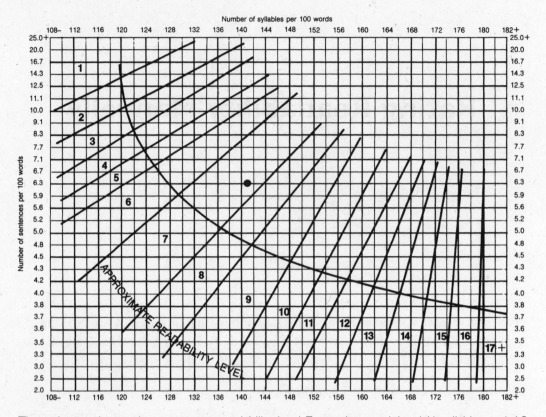

Number of syllables per 100 words

The point on the graph represents a readability level 7 sample containing 141 syllables and 6.3 sentences.

4. Plot your results. Find your sentence total on the vertical axis of the readability graph and your syllable total on the horizontal axis. Plot the point where the two lines intersect, and you'll see your document's readability level.

Calculate readability for several 100-word samples

Readability measurements are always rough approximations. It's an inexact method, so measuring one sample will not be enough. Plot the results of at least three samples, then estimate your readability level by averaging the three. When textbook editors rate a book, they assess samples from several chapters before arriving at a readability level.

Suggested Reading

Blumenthal, Joseph. *English 3200*, 4th ed. Cambridge, Mass.: International Thomson Publishing, 1994.

The Chicago Manual of Style: The Essential Guide for Writers, Editors, and Publishers, 15th ed. Chicago: University of Chicago Press, 1993.

Dumaine, Deborah, and the Better Communications® Team. *Instant-Answer Guide to Business Writing: An A–Z Source for Today's Business Writer.* Lincoln, Neb.: Writers Club Press, 2003.

Josephson, Judith Pinkerton, and Edith Hope Fine. *Nitty Gritty Grammar: A Not-So-Serious Guide to Clear Communication.* Berkeley, Calif.: Ten Speed Press, 1998.

Kilian, Crawford. *Writing for the Web* (Writers' Edition). Bellingham, Wash.: Self-Counsel Press, 2001.

Minto, Barbara. *The Minto Pyramid Principle: Logic in Writing, Thinking and Problem Solving.* London: Minto International, 1996.

O'Connor, Patricia T. *The Grammarphobe's Guide to Better English in Plain English.* New York: Riverhead Books, 1998.

Toor, Marcelle Lapow. *Graphic Design on the Desktop: A Guide for the Non-designer,* 2d. ed. New York: John Wiley & Sons, 1998.

Tufte, Edward R. *The Visual Display of Quantitative Information.* Cheshire, Conn.: Graphics Press, 2001.

Wilder, Claudyne, and Jennifer Rotondo. *Point, Click & Wow! A Quick Guide to Brilliant Laptop Presentations* (with CD-ROM). San Francisco: Jossey-Bass, 2002.

Wilder, Claudyne, and Jennifer Rotondo. *Slides That Win! Your Roadmap to Success* (an interactive CD-ROM). Santa Clara, Calif.: Crystal Graphics, 2001.

Williams, Robin. *The Non-Designer's Design Book: Design and Typographic Principles for the Visual Novice.* Berkeley, Calif.: Peachpit Press, 1994.

Zinsser, William. *On Writing Well,* 6th ed. New York: HarperCollins Publishers, 2001.

Index

and headlines, 37, 90
length of, 70, 74, 77, 89
linkages between, 60, 61, 62–63, 89, 90
purpose of, 60
revising/rewriting, 72, 196
and sales writing, 166
structure of, 90
and supportive criticism/critique, 196
and team writing, 196
transitions for, 60, 61, 62–63, 89, 90
and unity, 60, 90
and Web writing, 187, 188
parallel construction, 78–79, 148, 219–21, 253–54
passive voice, 91–95, 106, 240
patent applications, 53
performance appraisals, and sequencing, 52, 55, 207–8
personal profile graph, 247–48
personality, 30, 99
persuasion/influence
and challenges for writing, 5
and editing, 70, 71, 74, 76–77, 88, 101, 112
and positive approach, 112
and presentations, 136, 140, 142, 150
and proposals, 169–76
as purpose of writing, 13–14
and reports, 153, 155, 156, 157
and sequencing, 44, 45–46, 48, 55
and tone and style, 101
photographs, 74, 166, 188
planning
e-mail, 179–81
and organizing writing time, 58
for presentations, 122, 123
and team writing, 192, 201
and Web writing, 186, 189
See also specific step
planning reports, 52, 54
"point-by-point" order, 136
point of view, and reports, 156
position papers, team writing of, 191
positive approach, 71, 87, 112, 244–45, 260
Post-it notes
and grouping information, 34–35
as Start-up Strategy, 20, 25–26, 30
PowerPoint
and grouping information, 34

note pages, 129, 130, 147
and presentations, 25, 119, 120, 129, 130, 147
reports in, 120, 153–54
slides, 119, 124, 143
as Start-up Strategy, 20, 25, 27, 30
preface, in reports, 155
prepositions, 231
presentations
audience for, 119, 120, 122, 123, 124–29, 131, 132, 133
blueprint for, 120, 121–22, 130, 131–34, 135–36, 140, 148, 153
body of, 121, 134–40
checklist for, 123, 148, 150
close in, 122, 123, 140–42
components of, 121–22
and conclusions, 141–42
content for, 120, 123, 129–30, 135
daily documents compared with, 119–20
deciding which information to include in, 120
delivering of, 122, 123, 142–48
editing of, 70, 123, 148
Eight Steps to Audience-Centered, 120, 121, 122–50
and *Focus Sheet*, 122, 123, 124, 125–29, 131, 135, 143
generic, 120
goals/purposes of, 119, 121, 123, 124–29, 132, 133
and logistics, 126
modularized, 135–36, 138–39, 150
opening of, 121, 123, 131–34, 139
outlining and organizing, 121–22, 131, 134–42, 150
planning/preparation for, 122, 123, 147
and practice, 150
preview/agenda for, 121–22, 132, 134
rehearsing, 122, 123, 147, 148, 150
repetition in, 119, 120, 138, 148, 150
reports compared with, 120, 153, 154
sequencing in, 47, 54, 56, 57, 120, 123, 134–40, 145, 150
speeches compared with, 120
and Start-up Strategy, 25, 122, 123, 129, 130
strategies for, 126, 128–29, 150
visuals in, 121–22, 123, 138, 142, 150
Presenter's Blueprint, 120, 121–22, 130, 131–34, 135–36, 140, 148, 153

slides
  as handouts, 147
  and presentations, 122, 124, 130, 141, 142,
    143–44, 146, 147, 150
  and reports, 153
"So what?," 164–65, 171
solutions/recommendations
  benefits of, 171, 173
  in depth, 172, 174
  impact of, 171, 174
  and proposals, 171, 172, 173–74, 176
  and reports, 156, 158
  and sequencing, 45, 48, 52
spatial organization, 70, 73, 74, 79, 81, 89, 166–67.
    See also organization in space
speaker's notes, 122, 123, 142, 147, 150
specificity
  and editing, 87, 97–98
  of headlines, 40–41
  and M.O.D., 44, 55, 57
speeches, 120
spelling, 6, 71, 115, 116, 182
Start-up Strategy
  and blank-page/screen syndrome, 29–30
  and color coding, 22
  dictating as, 20, 29–30
  and distractions, 27
  and drafts, 65
  for e-mail, 22–23, 180, 181
  and editing, 88
  and *Focus Sheet*, 22, 30
  free screening as, 27–28
  free talking as, 29
  free writing as, 20, 26–28, 30
  to generate ideas, 19–30
  and grouping information, 34–37
  index cards as, 20, 25–26
  for letters, 22–23
  for memos, 22–26
  outlines as, 20–22, 23–25, 27, 30
  and personality, 30
  Post-it notes as, 20, 25–26, 30
  PowerPoint as, 20, 25, 27, 30
  and presentations, 122, 123, 129, 130
  for proposals, 23–25
  questioning as, 20, 22–23, 30
  and self-criticism, 26, 27

  and sequencing, 44
  as Step 2, 19–30
  and talking with others, 30
  and team writing, 194
  and Web writing, 187
  See also specific strategy
statistics, 57, 70, 138, 166, 187
status reports, 47
Step 1, 11–17. *See also* audience: analysis of;
    goals/purposes: defining
Step 2, 19–30. *See also* Start-up Strategy
Step 3, 31–42. *See also* grouping information;
    headlines
Step 4, 43–58. *See also* sequencing
Step 5, 59–67. *See also* drafts
Step 6, 69–116. *See also* editing
storyboards, 129–30
strategic reports, 57, 154
strategies
  and *Focus Sheet*, 14–15
  for presentations, 126, 128–29, 150
  and sales writing, 163
  and sequencing, 44, 49, 51
  and team writing, 193–94
  and triggering responses by letters, 211
  and writing as competive strategy, 168
  See also Start-up Strategy
streamlining, 70, 90–91, 106, 237–39, 257–58
structure
  and e-mail, 181, 182
  and editing, 70, 86–89
  of paragraphs, 90
  of reports, 159
  and Web writing, 187
style
  and criticism/critique, 199, 200
  and e-mail, 182
  and editing, 70, 71, 95, 99–114
  and team writing, 191, 194, 195, 197, 199, 200
  and Web writing, 186, 188
subject lines
  and drafts, 63
  and e-mail, 181, 182
  and editing, 106
  of proposals, 171
  and readability, 114
  and sequencing, 46